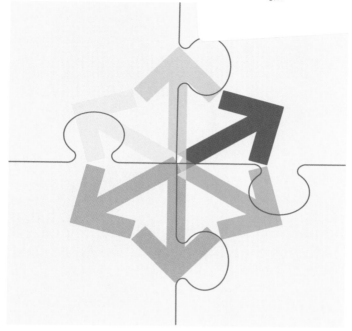

THE BUILDING BLOCKS OF
HIGH PERFORMING TEAMS

DAVE DAYMAN

First paperback edition printed in 2020.
A catalogue record for this book is available from the British Library.
Published by Successfactory Publishing, Chester, United Kingdom.
ISBN: 978-0-9931390-4-8
Illustrations by Martin Teviotdale.
The moral right of the author has been asserted.

"First, have a definite, clear practical ideal; a goal, an objective. Second, have the necessary means to achieve your ends; wisdom, money, materials, and methods. Third, adjust all your means to that end."

Aristotle 384-322BC

Foreword

Brigadier Leigh R Tingey

Deputy Commanding General, 1st (US) Armored Division (August 2018 - July 2020) and Commanding General Task Force Southeast, Afghanistan (July 2019 - April 2020)

I first met Dave Dayman in early 2006. A well-respected non-commissioned officer and communications and information management specialist, he joined the 150 strong unit of the Royal Engineers I was commanding, and we served together for the next 18 months. It was an incredibly demanding and busy period, which saw us exercise together in the United Kingdom, Canada and Kenya, and then deploy to Helmand Province in Afghanistan for 6 months. Dave, or Staff Sergeant Dayman as I referred to him back then, was an outstanding leader of his expert team of communication specialists. Exceptionally professional, impressively knowledgeable and utterly reliable, I trusted him implicitly and despite the numerous challenges we faced together in these extremely unforgiving training and operational environments, he never let me down. In every regard, he was a key member of my unit and was at the very heart of its success.

It was with great sadness, therefore, that a few years later I heard of his departure from the British Army. The Army's loss was undoubtedly the private sector's gain, and it was no surprise that I subsequently learnt of his ongoing success and the strong reputation he was building as a leadership and training consultant, most recently of course with Successfactory. Dave asked me to write the foreword for this wonderful book earlier this year during my most recent deployment to Afghanistan, this time commanding a 1500 strong Task Force of the US Army. It was an absolute honour and privilege to be asked and without hesitation I jumped at the opportunity.

Team Foundations is a 'must read' for anyone who aspires to be part of or lead a high performing team. I wholeheartedly agree with the key points raised in this book, all of which resonate with my own experiences of building, developing and leading high performing teams over the last 30 years. I've no doubt you'll find the six-building block structure as easy to follow as I did, namely: Culture and People; Strategy and Process; Truth and Trust; Knowledge and Decisions; Action and Mistakes; and Challenge and Support. Just as importantly, throughout the book these building blocks are clearly explained and ably brought to life by carefully selected team building and leadership tools, vignettes and visual examples.

One final comment. To reassure you; whilst my background is a military one, I have no doubt that Team Foundations is equally applicable to any high performing team scenario. I therefore unreservedly recommend it to you. It is extremely thought-provoking, will help you analyse your own contributions as either a team-player or leader, and will undoubtedly help you create the conditions needed for a high performing team to thrive. Read it, you will not be disappointed!

About the author

Dave Dayman is a Senior Training Consultant with the award winning Successfactory™.

His extensive knowledge about high performing teams and leadership has been built up over the years from working in the military, every sector in the civilian world and as a leadership and training consultant working with many of the world's leading brands.

Dave is a facilitator of thinking – he believes that thinking is not only the most powerful tool that we own but is also the one thing we have total control over, sometimes we just need a little help to change the way in which we choose to think. He is particularly adept at helping teams adopt a high performing culture but is also equally at home unlocking thinking in individuals to help them be the best that they can be.

Dave joined his first full-time working team in 1989 and from that point has operated in diverse areas and many teams, ranging from the UK Ministry of Defence, Engineering Specialists, long-range Communication Specialists, Training/Learning & Development departments, Senior Leadership teams and as an integral part of the world famous Successfactory™ training consultancy team.

He uses his extensive experience to design, deliver and support bespoke interventions that have real-life tangible benefits. These programmes include leadership, coaching, leading change, conflict resolution, and his specialty, which is helping create elite high performing teams.

Dave's hobbies and interests include camping and walking of which he has expedition experience. Dave is at his happiest when he is being challenged by the great outdoors and to relax, he likes to spend time working on his garden. Also, a keen guitar aficionado Dave enjoys the social interaction the music promotes as part of a rock band on the North West of England music scene.

The search for
purpose is always
more fruitful than
the search for
happiness.
Find the first
and the second
will follow.

Acknowledgements and thanks

Gemma for being you, your never-ending love, support and faith in me.

Graham Wilson for your professional and personal support, your endless enthusiasm for this topic and all your help in getting this book to print.

Leigh Tingey for writing the forward to this book and for teaching me what a great leader is and many things about working in a high performing team.

Martin Peterson for being a fantastic work colleague and a friend. You have an ability to level my thinking and your humour has lifted me many times.

Anne Wilson for your ongoing support – always in the background but always so vitally important.

Liane Orgill for your support and putting up with my sense of humour.

Steve Berry for your inspirational work and the fascinating conversations we have had about topics ranging from beetles to beer and your help with this book.

Phil Davies for your insights, stories, and inspirational conversations from the world of elite sport and for being a genuinely great guy.

James O'Brien for your honesty, sense of humour, your help and support.

Martin Teviotdale for the brilliantly creative artwork.

Josh and Abbie for putting up with 'the old man' and your unfaltering love.

Mum and Dad for, well...everything really!

All my family and friends who are so vitally important to me.

Contents

The beginning bit

The Chapters

The bit at the end

Section A

INTRODUCTION

What does the phrase teambuilding mean to you? Does it conjure up images of building a raft next to a windy lake with people you would rather not be spending your spare time with and getting wet? Well, it is much more than that...honestly!

It is exceedingly rare that a group of people who are randomly thrown together will instantly begin operating as a high performing team. In my 30 years of experience in leadership and teams it has become noticeably clear to me that there are several factors that need to be in place for a group of people to become a high performing team. It does not just happen – it takes work.

So why have I decided to write a book on this topic?

Throughout history there are examples of teams who have inspired others to follow a vision. High performing teams share a set of common fundamental characteristics. They are visionary, motivational, innovative and above all focused on working together towards a shared goal.

It is a topic that has fascinated me since I joined my first full-time team back in 1989. I thought I would ease my way into the world of work nice and gently by joining the Parachute Regiment! I later progressed to the Royal Engineers.

It has always amazed me how people operate together and how the interaction of people makes some teams good and others fall apart. I studied for a psychology degree in order to learn more about what makes people tick but if I'm honest, although I thoroughly enjoyed learning the topic and attaining my degree, I have learnt much more from just being immersed in teams, observing behaviours and how they corelate to results.

Many, many articles, blogs, presentations and books have been written on the topic of high performing teams and there are an abundance of 'experts' on hand to offer you their advice and 'this is how you do it' theories. So right from the off I'd like to make it clear that I do not consider myself an 'expert', I simply have my own experience of the subject and this book is just my own thoughts put to paper that I would like to share with you.

In the current, volatile, uncertain and forever changing world we need teams with tools, techniques, skills and, most importantly, a mind-set that is fit for purpose at all levels of an organisation to drive its transformational change forward.

This book is not intended to be an instruction manual or definite 'how to' guide. Anyone that knows me knows that I do not really do theory. I have built up a belief over the years that people can overuse theory and not use enough of their own real experience to shape their thoughts and ways of operating.

Sometimes people may use theory and jargon to over complicate things and baffle their audience/team/business in an attempt to hide the fact that they don't really necessarily have any tangible personal experience of the topic they are talking about or, perhaps, to appease their ego and seem more important or intelligent. Having said that, there are of course a few great theories out there that have stood the test of time with new ones being created every day. Theory has its place in creating conversation – the rest is practical application and adaptation.

My hope is that by sharing some of my own experiences and knowledge this book will help people with their team and leadership challenges by categorising the key traits that have worked in the past, and continue to work, to make teams successful with sustained high performance. These traits are what I have observed and studied when I have either led, been a member of, or worked remotely with teams in real time. From my early experiences of entering into the military world through to my experience of leading corporate teams to my most up to date experience working at the amazing Successfactory™, helping teams from all walks of life and every sector to be the best that they can be, has all fed into this book.

It is worth looking at this book as a conversation starter rather than a one-stop fix-all manual. There may be parts that you think, 'that is obvious' or, 'I know that, it's so simple'. That may be the case, but do you actually do it rather than just know it?

I have been extremely fortunate to have been gifted the opportunity throughout my working life to be both part of, and the leader of some exceedingly high performing teams. At times under extremely challenging conditions and on occasion, some rather less exciting ones. I am a realist and fully understand that not everything I say will resonate with everybody – the aim is for you to take away the bits that do resonate with you, adapt them, make them your own and most importantly apply them.

The book is laid out under 6 main chapters. Please feel free to dip in and out of the various chapters as you wish. You do not have to follow the book in a linear way. Each chapter is as equally important as the others. They are not in any order of priority. You can make your own minds up as to what your priorities are.

"No one can whistle a symphony; it takes a whole orchestra to play it."

Halford E. Luccock

Grab a drink of choice, have a notebook and pen to hand (or scribble in the book if that is your thing), find a place to relax, here we go...

Let us jump right in!

SAVoA Formation Skydiving Team
Glen Lowerson, Gareth Hicks,
Kim Myers, and Paul Myers.
Cameraman Pete Alexander.

6. Challenge & Support
1. Culture & People
5. Actions & Mistakes
2. Strategy & Process
4. Knowledge & Decisions
3. Truth & Trust

OVERVIEW OF TEAM FOUNDATIONS®

The model is interlinked and therefore each individual part relies on the success of the others and of course, each of them clearly has an impact on all the others.

Each topic will have its own dedicated chapter that will go into detail. I will use my own experiences and tie into theories where necessary to bring the headings alive. It is important that you link my words and experiences to your own world. Learn the main points and then connect them to your world. If you do not do this then you will not adapt them and then, importantly, apply them.

1. Culture & People

Create the right culture for your team and commit to a compelling Vision

Understand that people are different and use this to the team's advantage

2. Strategy & Process

Do not rely on long-term strategy planning

Have clearly defined, simple processes and get them 100% right but adapt them when necessary

3. Truth & Trust

Truth ALWAYS

Have trust in each other and in what happens when things don't go to plan

4. Knowledge & Decisions

Do not pretend to know everything

Use inclusive and flexible decision-making processes

5. Actions & Mistakes

Actions not just words

Have tolerance of mistakes

Do-Review-Understand

Strive to learn and keep moving forward

6. Challenge & Support

Challenge people but also give them permission to challenge back

Create an environment of mutual support

THE IMPORTANCE OF LEADERSHIP

"I think you have to rather
like people and realise
there is good in everyone
and as a leader you can
bring it out of them."

Captain Sir Tom Moore

Before we dive headfirst into the 6 main chapters (I know, you are keen to get going) it is worth quickly saying that leadership is a massive topic on its own and this book is not focusing solely on all the intricate details involved. (There is a plethora of books available that focus on leadership – I will put a list of recommended reading at the end of this book). That said, it is a vital component of a high performing team and the topics discussed in this book will not work as intended without strong leadership. Leadership no longer exists in the way it used to. The emphasis has shifted from the individual to a team leadership model. One person does not lead, it needs the collective diversity, knowledge, decision-making, challenge and support of a wider team.

> **"I'm the boss and therefore I am in control. I need to have the answers and I need to be consistent in my approach and the exact way I lead my team needs to continue via succession planning when I leave."**

A senior company director said the statement above to me a few years ago. How do you feel about it? Is that you or someone you know? Your boss maybe?

There are several areas of leadership that people struggle with – particularly in the early stages of their leadership journey as they set out to make their mark.

As a starting point I want to highlight three areas (the book will bring out others as we go through each chapter). Those three are control, continuity, and consistency. The 3Cs.

I recently coached/mentored someone who had the job title of Financial Controller. What do the words themselves conjure up in your mind? After a long discussion about what the person does, they decided that they would change the way they describe what they do. They do not control anything – what they actually do is help other people and the business by making their financial lives easier. So why is their job title not 'Director of making people's lives easier by doing all the numbers and finance stuff so you don't have to and allowing you to concentrate on your actual job' Pretty short and snappy job title, right?

We did have a laugh about job titles and came up with some quite funny ones [which I cannot put in this book]. We shared the opinion that job titles mean little to us both and what we really care about is what we actually do and the difference that it makes. In my experience, job titles rarely reflect what people do in real life on a day to day basis.

So, with that in mind, what do leaders do? What does the 'job title' of 'leader' mean to you? Stop for a moment and really give this some thought. Perhaps jot down some of your ideas to come back to.

Over the last few years, I have coached/mentored/helped many people who are both leadership veterans with a wealth of experience and others who are new to leadership. An area that a lot struggle with [particularly those new to leadership] is trying to be in control all the time. It wears them down very quickly and they get frustrated when they realise that they cannot control everything. They also cannot know everything and they for sure cannot be everything that everybody wants them to be all the time.

Here are 4 initial ideas for you to consider before you delve further into the book.

Keep coming back to these.

Idea
No

Stop trying to control everything.

You cannot and that is not what a leader [or any team member] does. What you can be is yourself and shout about your talents, skills and knowledge but also admit what you struggle with, what you are not so good at and when you need help. [More interesting stuff on this later]. Trying to be something or someone else is draining and eventually the cracks will appear on your façade and the real you will come to the surface. This usually happens when you are placed under stress/pressure. Things will crumble and this is what people will see. This is what your leadership will look like – cracked, false and unstable. This will reflect on the team and have a negative impact.

Idea
No

Do not get hung up with job titles.

Understand that leadership is not a job title – it is about being influential, motivational, engaging, inspiring, having empathy, asking questions, listening with the intent of understanding and above all – being human. All of this is to help move a team towards a shared goal, ambition, or mission.

During a recent coaching session with the aforementioned senior company director, we were discussing succession planning and that he felt it was imperative that someone is identified to take his role when he retires and that someone needs to be exactly like he is in order for there to be continuity. After a long chat about this he concluded that, for his direct team and the wider business, it would be more impactful if his successor was not like him in every way.

There will need to be some things that remain the same or similar of course, especially in the short-term to transition smoothly. Longer term however the 'new blood' could inject some very much needed new thinking and re-energise the team and business (more on this shortly – keep reading). In the modern world in which we work we must continue to challenge our thinking and allow ourselves and our teams to think differently. Things change too quickly and if leaders and senior leadership teams (and therefore the business) cannot think in an agile way then they are doomed to fail.

Idea
No

Continuity is both a helpful and a hindering thing.

I have witnessed many times the eager and dynamic team leader who has just been promoted to run a team and they jump straight in and try to change too many things. This is usually because they feel they must make an 'impact' and stamp their authoritative mark. Consider wisely what needs to remain and what needs to change in terms of how you lead a team.

This is particularly important if you are taking over as the leader of an already established team. So rather than changing everything for the sake of it or just continuing to do the same old thing because that is what you/the team have always done, really think about the few things that you could change that would have the biggest impact for the success of the TEAM.

Create a changeable, interactive, and agile culture that is constantly questioning how and why it does things. Culture is not fixed, and it is not something that you are detached from (chapter 1 goes into more detail about this). The things you do and say on a daily basis either change or perpetuate a culture. What impact are you making – good or bad, helpful or hindering?

However, contrary to the previous point, although leadership is about being agile and adapting to the needs of your team, your business and yourself, there are areas where consistency is also important. Giving appropriate and authentic praise is a good example of something that needs to be done consistently. Imagine if you as the boss came in on one day and were totally standoffish, unapproachable and cold but over the next two days you were happy-go-lucky, fun and all smiles? The day after that you were perhaps snappy and irritable.

How will this inconsistency make the team of people you lead feel? Uncertain, unclear, worried, guilty, angry themselves, upset perhaps or simply bemused.

Having a high level of emotional intelligence and understanding of who you are and how you come across in different situations, and with different people is a consistent that every leader needs and has a massive impact on the effectiveness of a team. A little later in the book there is an exercise that you can do to understand how you come across to others and help every member of the team get to know each other better.

Just remember that the way the boss comes in in the morning is the way that people go home at night.

Understand what absolutes you need to be consistent with.

Each member of your team will be different. They will need different continuity from you, and it is important that once you know individual preferences that you be that way – consistently.

The final point is to take into consideration the things that you do not need to control and let them go (feel the weight lift from your shoulders) – forget the continuity and consistency and try new things. You may be amazed with the results.

CHANGE – THE SAT NAV OF REALITY

During change we need DRIVERS who can DRIVE

Change is another topic that would need an entirely separate book to explore fully. The aim here is to scratch the surface and give you some ideas of things you can do to help with change in the context of building your high performing team.

How long does change take to happen? My answer to that question is – instantly. For example, an old policy or process finishes at 23.59 and the new one starts at midnight. The bit that most people call change is transition. It is the part after the actual change has taken place. You are transitioning from the old to the new and most of this happens in your mind.

"Change is not an event; it is a process triggered by an event. Some of these events are voluntary, some are imposed, and many just seem to happen. Regardless of the origin, the process that humans rely on to deal with them is what we call "change."

Daryl R. Conner

Change goes through predictable stages.

Think about it like going on a journey in the car. You switch the engine on, select the appropriate gear, accelerate, change gear when needed and then get to a nice cruising speed, you brake now and then, indicate when necessary until finally, you reach your destination. However, one thing that makes a journey less successful (or certainly less enjoyable) is traffic. How can you avoid it? Difficult in the UK in my opinion but just like any change/transition project you can plan and reduce the risks of 'traffic' affecting your journey.

Start to think about what traffic might hinder your journey to high performance. Your team's 'traffic' could be several things and I cannot tell you what your ' traffic' is, but in my experience of developing teams, it is likely to include several of my top 10:

1. **Fear of something new**
2. **Fear of failure**
3. **Fear of success (if it works well I/we will be given more work to do)**
4. **Lack of breadth of skills across the team**
5. **Previous experiences of change that was not handled well**
6. **Poor leadership**
7. **Clash of egos and agendas**
8. **No clarity about the purpose of the team**
9. **Ineffective recruitment leading to the wrong people in the team**
10. **People not 'walking the talk', particularly with values**

You will need to explore this as a team and constantly evaluate it. It needs to be in your risk assessment.

Successful transition involves planning. For those participating, this includes a lot of activity and work; to the rest of the organisation, it can seem like nothing is actually happening. All change initiatives, whether a business change project, or building a new team have at least one stretch of 'traffic', the time when momentum levels off (or stops completely).

Transition can fail at any stage and for various reasons, but the 'traffic' is always the critical turning point. When allowed to go on for too long, a change project can take a turn off toward failure. If you take the wrong turn early in the journey of your high performing team creation it can be exceedingly difficult and take a long time to get back on to the main road again. Especially if you are not even sure where that road is going to end up (vision).

Failure often occurs when leaders and team members lose focus or become involved in other interesting new initiatives – the next new shiny thing! They may even assume that decreasing results mean the change is not working and pull the plug. If you are changing your team culture, then it is imperative that this change project happens before you move on to other shiny things. Building the team for sustained success is your ONLY priority at this stage and using the 6 chapters outlined in this book will help to set you up for success in the long run rather than some potentially easier short-term quick wins.

As we will explore in later chapters, planning is important, but you will not avoid 'traffic' completely, no matter how well you plan. What you can do is have systems and processes in place, plus a mind-set and culture in your team that stops it lasting too long and threatening the long-term success of the team. Know when and how to turn off and re-route.

Try doing these things:

- Analyse the bigger picture before you start your journey to identify potential 'traffic spots' that will become barriers to team progress and ultimate success; for example, a team member's focus shifting elsewhere, too many simultaneous initiatives, or fatigue from the change. Perhaps look at other teams to see what worked for them and what did not. What 'traffic' held them up?

- Select the right gear for the start of your team build journey so it does not stall from the off. People are different and the speed that you like to operate at may not suit every team member. Get the right balance and do not simply drag people along with you.

- Decide on key actions that will build steady acceleration and create a realistic timeline to sustained high performance.

- Do not fudge the paperwork/reporting side of things to imply that the change is complete, either by declaring success prematurely or by making it seem as though it failed. Be honest always! Creating a high performing team takes time and is not just a tick box exercise. It also takes a lot of effort but do not give up!

- Be prepared to change your journey. Not the destination, which should have been thoroughly thought through and well planned and is where you need to be. Listen to the sat nav of reality – if it's telling you things are not working and there is traffic then change direction.

Remember small actions can sometimes have as great an impact as big ones. A small win is still a win – celebrate it. The most effective sustainers of behaviour change all invest their time and resources where the impact is. We buy into change when we can feel, see, hear, and touch it personally. If the effect is good for us, then we buy-in. Find the advantages no matter how small for you and the team rather than allowing people to look solely at the negative aspects of the change.

Another reason that change can be difficult is because it is human nature to become attached to the way things are. Psychologically, we do not like to switch from something that is working well for us and makes us feel comfortable to something new. This is partly due to the way the brain works. Our brains often operate in survival mode and want to keep us safe and therefore, our inclination is to stay in our comfort zone. We also all have emotional ties to the status quo. If something has an emotional attachment for you then you are less likely to want to change it. For example, if the first team you ever worked in was a positive experience for you; that first boss was a very positive influence and the way that the team operated really resonated with you and you had great results, you would have created an emotional bond with both the people and the team culture.

Move forward 20 or 30 years and these older ways of working may not work in your current climate. Breaking that emotional bond with the old can be difficult but is sometimes essential.

A rather simple example of this that I have encountered recently is changing my car. I had been driving the same car for many years and really liked it. It still looked ok, drove ok as far as I was concerned and was just comfortable like an old pair of shoes. However, for various reasons I had to get a new car that ended up being a bit different from my old, familiar one. How did it feel? Exciting? Yes, but also quite daunting. One thing is for sure, my driving became slower. More on my car later. I am sure that you can think of your own experiences and examples of emotional attachment and how it has affected you during change.

Do not forget that the actual timeline of change/transition is a challenge. A team will (should) discuss and create an amazing vision and then start to put in motion the wheels of this change/transition. The discussions and planning can take a long time and should always involve all team members. This will reduce their own internal resistance to the change (or aspects of it).

What you need are excellent DRIVERS on a change journey

In a world of constant change, ambiguity, complexity, and uncertainty people can be scared. It is important that leaders see their role is to ensure people feel safe and secure and that they plan change/transition effectively. Once you do that, those that follow may surprise you.

There are four key elements to think about when making change happen

1. **D**issatisfaction with current **R**eality
2. **I**nspirational **V**ision
3. **E**asily **R**ecognisable **S**teps
4. Capability for **Change**

This is taken from the Drivers for Change Model which can be found in the brilliant book, Leadership Laid Bare™ by Graham Wilson. I will briefly run through it here and I highly recommend reading the entire book.

The Change Equation is fundamental to understanding the components and psychology of change and provides a helpful starting point in thinking about leading and achieving successful change. The key with this model is to establish a credible plan that considers all four elements. No individual element takes priority – they all need to be in place, so do not think you will save time by choosing the one(s) that resonate the most with you or perhaps the ones that look easiest to implement.

Look at them all in equal measure.

Dissatisfaction with the current Reality

The first thing to consider is the Dissatisfaction with the current Reality. What is the current reality and how much is it affecting those involved? You can only plan an effective change initiative if you are tackling areas that create dissatisfaction. If this is not the case, then you need to ask why you are doing it in the first place.

Sometimes we are unaware of dissatisfaction until we are made aware of something that could potentially be better. Back to my car again – I did not have any major dissatisfaction with my old car, I felt comfortable with it, like I said. That was until I saw an amazing deal on a newer car that had a few more shiny things that would benefit me, like a built in DAB radio for example. Suddenly, I was a little dissatisfied with the old and started to consider the new.

Inspirational Vision

With change and transition you need to create an Inspirational Vision of what will be. It is so important to consider how are you going to communicate and sell this vision to all those involved and impacted? Or better still, how will you involve them in creating an inspirational vision? People are not opposed to change nearly as much as they are opposed to change that they did not think of or were not involved in planning. Interestingly, buy-in happens most fully when people understand the why, rather than the what or how. A little later in this chapter I will share some ideas that might help you when creating the vision for your team.

Easily Recognisable Steps

Sometimes change can be made too complex. It is a fact that people are more likely to buy into change if it has been broken down into easily recognisable steps. Chapter 2 explores why this break down approach should also be considered when creating processes in a team.

Complexity can baffle people – simple steps look less scary and more achievable. Think about chunking the big stuff down into bite-sized, manageable steps on a realistic 'drumbeat' timeline.

Capability for Change

People do (or do not) do things for two main reasons. Firstly, because they can – they have the ability, and, secondly, because they want to – they are motivated. Therefore, it is important that those impacted by any change initiative have the capability for change. If the capability is not there, what can you do, as a team, to change that?

It is worth noting that both the 'can do' (ability) and the 'want to do' (the motivation) aspects are vital – therefore, at this stage concentrate on both the technical and the psychological aspects. Just because a person or a team has the technical capability for change, it does not mean that they are necessarily motivated for it. More on motivation later.

The goal that you are looking for is real change to a culture that will allow high performance in your team. This means inclusive change as opposed to forced change.

"If you want to build a ship, don't drum up the men to go to the forest and gather wood, saw it, and nail the planks together, but rather teach them to long for the endless immensity of the sea."

Antoine de Saint-Exupéry

Change can still take place if certain elements are missing from the DRIVERS CAP model, but it will be less impactful. The aim is to really analyse all the four areas and identify actions for each element. If you plan effectively you are much more likely to establish real (sustainable) change of your team culture that team members buy in to.

Finally, do not lose sight of everything because of the end goal – yes that needs to be well thought out, realistic and attainable (and attractive) but never at the expense of how you get there.

"It is good to have an end to journey towards; but it is the journey that matters, in the end."

Ursula K LeGuin

So far, I have mentioned the word team quite a lot. That is going to happen in a book about high performing teams, so it is perhaps worth stopping for a moment to consider what a team is. Before you read any further, write down a few ideas of your own. What does 'team' mean to you?

WHAT IS A TEAM?

Here is one definition from the business directory:

A group of people with a full set of complementary skills required to complete a task, job, or project.

Team members [1] operate with a high degree of interdependence, [2] share authority and responsibility for self-management, [3] is accountable for the collective performance, and [4] work toward a common goal and shared reward[s]. A team becomes more than just a collection of people when a strong sense of mutual commitment creates synergy, thus generating performance greater than the sum of the performance of its individual members.

It is a great definition but there are a lot of factors there! So, where do we start? An uncomplicated way of explaining it is to say that a team is a collection of people who work together and support each other to achieve a shared goal. Or, put another way:

A Group:

- A collection of individuals who see themselves as members of the same social category.
- Perform and function as individuals. Concentrate on their own specialisms and areas of expertise.
- Are individually accountable for their own work outputs.
- Will come together when encouraged to share information, make decisions, and help individuals achieve their goals.
- Have meetings that remain too structured and rigid and are usually pointlessly ineffective.
- Tends to have (need) strong directive leadership.
- Discuss, decide, delegate, but everyone tends to want to sculpt the discussions towards their own area of responsibility.

A Team:

- Has individual and mutual accountability for all aspects of the team's output.
- Come together to achieve collective goals.
- Understand that the sum is greater than the individual parts.
- Have open ended and active decision-making meetings when needed.
- Have a self-defined team purpose.
- Use shared leadership with no egos getting in the way.
- Discuss, decide, work together. Shifts language from 'I' to 'we' or 'us'.

There are a lot of things to think about and the list is not exhaustive. I am sure you have already added your own ideas. If not, take a moment to make some notes. I always encourage people to do this when I am coaching or mentoring. Everyone is different but, notes can help you consolidate and organise your thoughts and they give you something to come back to rather than simply forgetting the things that come into your head.

This book should help you continue to build on your ideas.

As I mentioned, I tend not to use copious theory, but some of you may have spotted ideas drawn from elements by people such as Kellerman, Katzenbach & Smith and Tuckman so far. To give an option for those who would appreciate an on-line evaluation to establish the extent to which you are working in a GROUP or a TEAM or a High Performing Team, my good friends at EvaluationStore.com have offered a free of charge evaluation to every purchaser of this book (normally £9.99 per team member). Their evaluation reports also dive deeper into the work of the authors and researchers mentioned above.

With an EvaluationStore.com High Performing Team (HPT) evaluation, each team member evaluates the team against 20 key criteria and a consolidated report shows (anonymously) how the whole team measures. The team can then decide which criteria they should concentrate on to develop further and then formulate plans to do so. If requested, the team at SuccessFactory™ can help you with this process.

If you want to take advantage of this offer from EvaluationStore.com then:

1. **Visit www.EvaluationStore.com and look at sample reports of the HPT evaluation.**

2. **Use the 'Contact' section on the EvaluationStore.com homepage to alert them that you would like to set up and complete a free of charge evaluation. Include this information:**
   a. Mention that you are reading 'Team Foundations' (it won't be free of charge unless you do).
   b. Say what your company/business/organisation name is
   c. Say the name of the team you want to evaluate, one team only.
   d. Say how many people are in that team (up to 15 people)

3. **Using the e-mail address you give, EvaluationStore.com will contact you and either show you how to set up the free of charge evaluation yourself (this is the recommended option as you then keep control and can revisit results whenever you choose), or EvaluationStore.com would be prepared to set it up for you.**

4. **You get a 'code' and instructions which you pass on to every team member.**

5. Each team member cuts & pastes the code into the box on the EvaluationStore.com homepage and it takes them to the evaluation of your team.

6. Each team member completes the evaluation and gets a PDF report of their own inputs.

7. When all have completed it, you download a consolidated report PDF.

8. You have a tangible report of the areas of HPT strengths and weaknesses, plus recommendations and analysis to discuss.

9. You and your team can meet (with or without development experts such as SuccessFactory™) to determine where you should focus to improve your team and how you should do this.

10. You start implementing your action plan and move closer towards being a High (or Even Higher!) Performing Team.

The foundations of team success

I recently delivered a senior leadership development programme to a high-level building regulations company in the UK. Not only was this a fantastic learning journey for the leaders involved, it was also an eye opener for me. I learnt more about the intricacies of the building industry, and more specifically, knowledge about how houses are built than I ever imagined existed. It got me thinking that putting a high performing team together is a bit like constructing a building. Firstly, you need to establish the purpose and function of the building before you put it together. Is it a family home, if so, how many bedrooms? Perhaps it is a business unit, warehouse, or an office. Let us use the example of a house.

A properly built house (and any building of course) is only as good as its foundations – without a sturdy and durable base it would simply crumble and fall when exposed to time and external pressures. Although there are several ubiquitous elements that are critical to all building foundations (bases), the finished supports will not be 100% identical. The foundations for buildings in areas prone to earthquakes for example are different to say the standard foundations found in UK homes. They need to be different as they need to cope with different situations. The foundations of a team are the same.

Therefore, it is imperative that you understand why your team exists – what its purpose is and in what context and situations you operate. If you do not know this, then how can you build the correct foundations?

It is significant to point out that the foundations of a high performing team are generally not the fancy exciting things that people often say are the traits of high performing teams (the lovely looking building above the ground) but are the simple processes and procedures that have been agreed and consistently applied and adapted. (More on processes in chapter 2).

Teams, like buildings need a strong bond between the bricks (people) to keep together. Again, this is back to the basics – get simple procedures in place and let each 'brick' understand its place and how important it is to the strength and integrity of the entire building and the wider impact it has.

Just as each building may have several specialist rooms, utility, kitchen, bedroom etc., each business/team has separate sub-departments or specialisms, but they all contribute to the whole. Without the input of each – it simply does not work as it is meant to.

Buildings do not just happen though, even with the best builders. What is needed is the skill and vision of an architect. So perhaps that is another way of looking at what leadership is?

CHAPTER 1. CULTURE & PEOPLE

● Create the right culture for your team and commit to a compelling Vision

● Understand that people are different and use this to the team's advantage

"Have the courage to see what is wrong with your culture and then do something about it."

Dave Dayman

What do I mean by culture? It is one of those words that gets banded around a lot, especially in the corporate world. It is certainly up there in the top five things that clients talk to me about when they approach me for help (along with lack of effective communication, inflexibility of processes, lack of bonding in the team and struggling with problem solving and strategy planning). So why is culture such a buzz word?

Well, firstly you **should not** consider it as just a buzz word. It is the absolute bedrock of a successful team/business. Culture is a 360-degree, organic thing. It is made up of individual and collective behaviours, the myriad of micro-languages used during interactions and conversations, the psychological contracts between employer and employee, the ritual habits that you observe and the 'brand' of who you are as a unit. You are not separate from it, you cannot point at it and say 'that is the culture over there' – you are immersed in it and the things that you do every day either change or perpetuate the culture you are in. This goes for every member of a team. Culture is partly made up of history – what has been before and that is either changed or perpetuated by you, the team members. The actions and behaviours that you choose to adopt make your culture what it is.

If the culture you have is not working for you then only you (the team) can change it. No excuses! I have heard hundreds of times that, 'we don't have time', 'it's not my/our job', 'there is too much resistance from above', etc., etc...THESE ARE ALL EXCUSES! If building a high performing team is your goal, then let go of these excuses and start acting – take action! (More about taking action in chapter 5).

The recruitment process is the vital first step in building a high performing team. Now this might seem obvious, but it never fails to amaze me how many organisations still get this wrong. Your business and team may be attacking innovative thinking and stifling high performance (not to mention morale) through a lack of clarity and communication between the business/team need and the recruitment process.

Before recruiting for your new team (or moving people around internally if re-jigging your existing team) establish the POINT of the team. I cannot emphasise this enough! This really needs some thought – do not just write down a load of corporate words. It is all well and good putting lots of thought and effort into recruiting amazing people who are highly skilled AND have the right mind-set etc., but why are you doing that? What is the point? The first thing is to establish your purpose.

"Management has a lot to do with answers. Leadership is a function of questions. And the first question for a leader always is: 'Who do we intend to be?' Not 'What are we going to do?' but 'Who do we intend to be?'"

Max DePree

1. Why is this team being set up or the current team being changed?

2. What outcomes are you/the business/the organisation looking for?

3. What difference do you/the team want to make? (Go above and beyond the business/corporate strap lines).

4. Is the purpose desirable and feasible? Is the purpose really needed in the business?

5. Do you believe in it?

Perhaps jot down some initial ideas. Whatever comes into your head get down on a piece of paper. Do not judge your thoughts, just capture them.

Once you have consolidated your own thoughts it would be advantageous for you to take the time to sit down with your team, if you already have one in place, and discuss the previous questions before you get too far into this book. The answers that you come up with will serve you well as a guide, a road map if you like, to help keep you on track during the journey of creating YOUR high performing team.

Below is an interesting exercise to help you capture some ideas about where you need to be.

The Imagined Future

Imagine you are at a point in the future where you have built your team or achieved all the team improvements that you set out to do. Your team has been identified as a high performing team. All the key performance measures around business performance and people are truly at the top of their game with consistent delivery. Team members are individually and collectively successful and they are also happy.

You are about to deliver a 5-minute presentation to the CEO and Senior Leadership team, summarising in no more than a page of A4 the key ingredients which are at the heart of your high performing team.

What will you say?
Take the time now to write this down. As Covey said, "Start with the end in mind".

Keep these notes. You do not need to over analyse at this stage, it is simply good to have a starting point. As you go through the book come back to these initial ideas and adapt them, as necessary. You have created the bones – the skeleton of your idea for success, so now let us put some meat on those bones.

Stage 4: HOW?

More meat is added to the bones at this stage – the more intricate detail of how things will get done to achieve the goals and purpose. Agreed processes, roles, standards and values are the key. You could call this a set of guiding principles that define how you will achieve your goals. [More on guiding principles a little later]. If people are not clear on the 'how' it will cause silos, separate agendas, and disharmony.

Stage 5: WHO, WHAT, WHEN and WHERE?

This stage is about timing and scheduling, being clear on who does what and when. This will tie into your processes and procedures and adds even more detail. Whether you love or hate them, processes are vitally important to a high performing team. Without them things can descend into chaos rather rapidly. As we will explore later, it is imperative you have clearly defined, simple processes and you get them 100% right but also have the ability and mind-set to adapt them when necessary.

Stage 6: MAINTAINING, REVIEW AND MOVE

This is about sustained energy and synergy. Once a team achieves success it is not the end.

The final stage is about using effective review tools to ensure that you are still matching your actions to the purpose, goals, and strategy in line with any external factors. A team cannot afford to simply sit back and just 'do' without continued thought about possible ways to do things better/more efficiently etc. A high performing team has tools, techniques, frameworks, and processes in place that help them to anticipate future changes and adapt to necessary change. This ensures that the team sustains high performance and success.

Success does not stagnate – it moves.

A team must review regularly to capture what it is doing well and to flexibly respond to goal changes, it is also important to celebrate successes together. This helps you to carry on doing what is working well and decide what things you are going to do differently. We will explore later in this book the need for high performing teams to continually challenge and support each other.

At each of the stages it is imperative that you achieve a level of harmony in the team. Do not move forward if areas are unresolved. You will only have to come back to it later and by then, it will be harder to fix.

Using these stage ideas is still very relevant in the context of changing an existing culture as opposed to building one from scratch – it's just a bit harder (but you are up for the challenge I can just tell).

When it comes to creating a culture, many businesses get far too bogged down in corporate speak and objectives (numbers usually). Sadly, it becomes all about KPIs. Someone once told me that KPI stands for 'kick people intensely', which is sadly pretty accurate.

Let us take a different view of culture creation. Have you ever watched children play? It is quite incredible to watch! The amazing intricacies of the story lines they create, the diversity of the characters and the boundless energy and lack of regard for boundaries or parameters. What children are particularly good at (in my opinion) is being able to fully immerse themselves in the scenarios that they create - they become part of the story. The interesting thing for me is that the children also create sets of values and a culture within their story (generally they do not use that language - they just do it). They then act out their play/scenario and live within their created values (and usually enjoy themselves at the same time). My point (and question) is, when do we stop doing that? It is the norm when children play for them to create a storyline (ambition, strategy, vision, goal), they create social and cultural norms around their story (values, rules, principles), and then actually live these values (most of the time) whilst having fun! Not only that, when a child stops playing (usually because an adult has told them to), in their head they are still in character and generally continue to behave in that way.

Thinking back to my own childhood (which was far too long ago) I can recall being called back in for an evening meal after playing out in the woods all day and I was still Robin Hood.

Wouldn't it be great if businesses adopted this more free-flowing approach and team members were that involved in the team's 'story'? (Some organisations have nailed this of course but not many). Let us go back to childhood and be authentic again. Remind ourselves of the power of PLAY and create an amazing story (vision) for your business that is exciting. Put in place values and principles that mean something and that you are actually going to live by and please, don't forget the **FUN** part.

My colleague and friend at Successfactory™, Martin Peterson, runs some brilliantly engaging sessions using Lego Serious Play™. Martin has kindly let me sit in on some of his sessions and they never fail to amaze me – they are powerful. I have seen him take senior leadership teams who turned up very stiff and corporate with reams of paperwork wanting help with the creation/adaptation of their vision and culture to a place where they were using Lego to create the vision. Linking into the core theme 'main' build there were many separate satellite builds that showed the shared values, strategies and behaviours. The teams had a visual and fun representation of what can be a very dull, corporate creation process. Like I said, do not forget the power of fun, even if you are a senior team in the corporate world! At Successfactory™ we call it fun with a serious intent. It is a very liberating feeling once the ties are loosened (or preferably off) and a team start to talk and act together on a human level and are not shrouded in corporate nonsense.

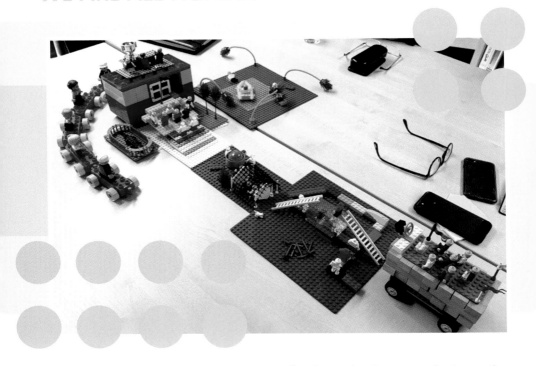

If you already have a culture in your team/business that is not conducive to the ideas contained in this book, then you will need to strip it back and re-build it in a systematic way. This is the whole unfreeze, change and re-freeze idea. This takes time and you will meet resistance. People get used to what they know and rarely like change.

The importance of knowing who the team is and the culture you want.

Here are some things that you can do as a team to link individuals to the team culture. They are not easy but persevere.

The most powerful thing that a team can do is talk. Talk about why the team exists, what do they do? What values underpin what they do? What drives everyone? (Honestly – not just mindlessly spouting the corporate line).

What does each person contribute to the team? What are the things that people do that hinder the team? And what does success look and feel like for every single member of the team and then as a collective? And you will potentially need to talk about why things need to change.

Everybody is different and you need to know these differences and be able to align them in a team so that you are using them to your advantage. It is also important to ask whether people are genuinely happy.

These types of conversations can be difficult to get going but I have found that once a team realises that everyone is human and that it is a safe environment, they open up more and start talking honestly. A good way to open a conversation is to start by talking about real life outside of work.

Each team member is the gatekeeper of their own thoughts and information and is free to divulge as much or as little as they wish. Life is not all about work and the external aspects of team member's lives will have a big impact on the internal operation of the team. Talking and sharing makes this impact easier to deal with and allows every team member to adjust how they operate according to the pressures on others. Talking about non-work stuff is also human and humans need social interaction.

This social interaction is likely to make people feel more comfortable talking about more difficult issues in a work context. Once the team get to know each other a little better you should observe more open and honest conversations. That is when you can introduce more challenging conversations to tackle team issues.
The following exercise is an example of a facilitated discussion that you can adapt as necessary and use.

You will need time and head space to do this properly!
Ensure that you are in a comfortable and relaxed place. No other distractions, no phones, no laptops and with plenty of refreshments on hand.

Ask each member of the team (including you) to write down their own individual answers to the following questions:

1. **Why does the team exist?**

    ....
    ....
    ....

2. **What do the team do?**

    ....
    ....
    ....

3. **What values underpin what they do?**

    ....
    ....
    ....

4. **What drives them individually?**

    ....
    ....
    ....

5. **What do they contribute to the team?**

    ....
    ....
    ....

6. What are the things they do that hinder the team?

7. What does success look and feel like to them?

8. Are they (and you) happy?

Do not rush this and make it clear that honesty is crucial.

Now invite each team member to write down three words or short phrases that they think sum themselves up as a person. This is just high level and does not need to be an essay.

For example, someone might write 'I care – I like to know people are ok', 'I am stubborn', 'I get anxious about meetings' etc.

These thoughts must be how you really feel you are and not what you want other people to think you are.

So, at this stage, each team member will have their own piece of paper with answers to the initial questions and three words/short statements that summarise who they feel they are, and how they come across to others. Allow everyone to keep their thoughts to themselves at this stage and ask them all (including you) to put that piece of paper away – keep it safe, you will come back to it in a bit.

Here comes the more challenging bit.
Ask every team member to write down three words or short phrases/statements that sum up every other person in the team. Put one word or phrase on a single Post-it so you will end up with three Post-its per team member (you can do more if you wish).

Be professional but completely honest – how do they really come across to you?

Allow people the time and space to do this. You can even spread out to different rooms/areas or do it virtually.

Once everyone is ready, hand the Post-its out to the respective team members. You will probably get a mixture of laughing (nervous and genuine humour), gasps, smiles, frowns, and the odd expletive! Let everyone read and absorb the words/phrases/statements and ask them to also categorise them, i.e., if people have put the same or similar, then put these Post-its together.

Now ask them to take out the piece of paper with their thoughts about themselves that they previously scribbled down and look at how well their own words and phrases correlate with what the rest of the team have said about them.

Each team member should end up with two piles of Post-its (keep this high level and simple) – pile one consists of the Post-its from others that match (or are close to) what they have said about themselves. Pile two consists of the Post-its from others that do not match how they feel about themselves.

The bigger the first pile the better. This means that you are more aware of who you are and how you come across to others. You are being authentic.

Now open some wider discussions. Initially it may be useful to let people mingle about and ask individuals to clarify what they mean and to expand on their Post-it points. Then come together as a full team to discuss thoughts. This will need to be controlled as it can easily get out of hand and key points lost. I always find it a good idea to capture thoughts on a large white board or flip charts. No filter, no analysis at this stage and no judgment – simply capture it all.

During the whole team discussion invite and encourage everyone to ask other team members questions like:

What makes me seem that way to you?

What actions do you observe in me that make you feel that way?

How does this impact you and make you feel?

What impact do you think my actions have on the team dynamic?

It is important to do this openly with everyone listening to every question so that you can validate comments. For example, if one person in a team says that you come across as quite angry but no one else really sees this then it is clearly an issue with just that one person and can be dealt with in a separate conversation. If, however several people say that they also see that trait in you then this is an area to be explored in more detail as a team.

Now come back to the initial questions; why does the team exist? What do they do? What values underpin what they do? What drives them individually? What does success look and feel like to them? Are they happy? And openly discuss all of these as a whole team.

Look for correlation and discrepancies.
You will see that there will be areas that people agree on and others that are further apart. For the team to be successful you need to bridge those gaps. For example, if the reason that the team exists or what success looks like are different to different people then how do you formulate a strategy and plan to get there? [More on this later].

This can be a long session but let it run (it may take many sessions to do this fully). Keep it professional and if it seems to be getting a bit heated take a break.

The aim of doing this challenging exercise is to find out how each of you comes across to other members of the team and the impact that everyone has on the wider team.

When I run these sessions, I usually observe that they start off negatively as human nature (particularly in the corporate world) seems to default towards the highlighting of negative traits and behaviours. Given a bit more time and facilitated discussion you will find that more positive things start to emerge. People can say some amazingly powerful things about the positive impact that individuals have on them and interestingly, those individuals (or the wider team) had no idea that this was the case.

You will hopefully quite quickly see the dynamic and mood change as the team discussions progress. People become more animated, involved and sometimes more emotional. This is all good – let it happen and do not fight it. Perhaps even add in extra time for people to chat to whoever they like over a coffee and talk on a human level, about family, hobbies, passions, dislikes, mistakes, relationships, work – anything that immerses them in dialogue at a human level rather than surface level stuff.

It is always fascinating watching body language when people talk about things that they are passionate about – they light up and you can feel and see their positive emotion.

It is also interesting to see how the listener changes. In my experience, when the conversation goes below just surface level and has emotional meaning then the listener is genuinely curious to hear more and listens properly.

"Listen with curiosity. Speak with honesty. Act with integrity. The greatest problem with communication is we do not listen to understand. We listen to reply. When we listen with curiosity, we do not listen with the intent to reply. We listen for what's behind the words."

Roy T. Bennett,
The Light in the Heart

I will make no bones about it; these type of team sessions can be hard (specially to start with) but the open and honest approach is vital if the team are to succeed together in the long run. As Bob Hoskins once said, "it's good to talk". It creates a culture of openness and honesty and it will help you all align to your vision.

"Leadership is the capacity to translate vision into reality."

Warren Bennis

What is a vision in a business context?

Have you ever been on a train and the driver does not know where they are going? No, me neither...or at least I am hoping that was the case and not just blind luck that I ended up where the information board said the train was going. To get to the correct destination a train driver, the crew and train company need a vision and a plan to keep people on track (pun intended).

And let us not forget that a single train journey is part of a much bigger network. In today's world of continuous demands there is a requirement for leaders and teams to move quickly and effectively between numerous tasks ensuring that they align to the bigger picture. All these separate tasks need to feed into an overarching vision.

The vision is your guide

I have put together a set of questions that team members can answer individually and then share with the wider team. This should generate an interesting discussion – it is a brilliant conversation starter that begins to explore areas that your team and/or business could improve on and things that you are currently doing that are working. Or, if you are a newly formed team then this can help set the vision that will work for you.

Here are the first 14 questions (feel free to add your own):

1. What is a vision and what is it intended to do?

2. What is the link between vision, mission, strategy, goals, and objectives?

3. Which organisation do you believe 'lives by' a set of values and behaviours, which are instantly recognisable? If you are not sure what their stated values are just look them up.

4. What do these values say about the team/organisation?

5. What do you think it would be like to work there? What makes you say that?

6. Would you be a customer/client? If so, why?

7. What approach do/did the leader or leaders of this organisation take?

8. Was it good or bad leadership in your opinion? Expand on what you mean by good and bad leadership when you do this.

9. What is your team's/business's vision and what do you think of it?

10. In line with this vision, what behaviours are expected of you?

11. Is your vision compelling, inspirational, and well known both internally and externally? (Something for you to consider – if I were to approach any member of your team/organisation and asked them to articulate the business/team vision, could they?)

12. What do your customers, clients, the public or your competition say about your team/business? If you do not know what people honestly say about you – why not?

13. What can you do as a team/business to be more like the 'great' organisations that you have identified?

14. How could you possibly capitalise more on the things that you are already doing well?

Now identify an organisation who you believe behaved in ways that were opposite to their stated values. You might want to think about current news headlines.

Here are the next 5 questions:

1. What were the stated values of this organisation?

2. What did they do that ran opposite to these stated values?

3. What impact do you believe this had on the organisation's...?
  a. Workforce?
  b. Customers/clients?
  c. Reputation?

4. Again, look at what approach the leader or leaders of this organisation took. Was it good or bad leadership in your opinion? Expand on this.

5. What can you learn about your own leadership, team, and organisation from answering the previous questions?

If you have not done so already then now is a great time to come back together as a full team to continue the discussion. How many team members chose the same organisation? What does this tell you? What are the similarities between individual choices? Analyse the differences in opinion and what this might mean for your team.

Summary – Culture

Many teams continue with a culture because it is simply 'how we operate around here'. It is great to have ways of working that are based in the traditions of your organisation as this helps to cement a feeling of pride (the military thrive on this), but, the world now is a forever changing thing so a team cannot simply rely completely on the old traditions and ways of operating – it needs to adapt and be flexible to keep up with the world we now operate in.

Ask what is your current reality and where do you want/need to be?

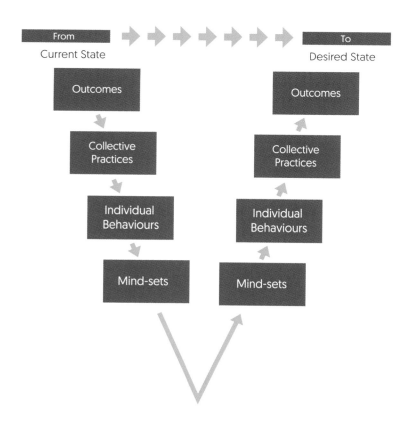

The knowledge we had yesterday was fit for purpose then, but is it now?

> # "When you stop expecting people to be perfect, you can like them for who they are."
>
> ## Donald Miller

People make a team

The simplest and most common way of describing a person is to identify patterns of behaviour and to label them with trait names (introverted, happy, moody, helpful etc). But who states what constitutes a trait? Whose definition is 'happy' or 'helpful'? There are some who may say that this process of categorising people is simply a case of naming but not explaining! A mood can be characteristic of a person over time and friendliness can be a temporary disposition instead of an enduring trait. We tend to try to fit people into categories according to our cultural norms and our own ideas but are our perceptions and consequent categorisations really about the other person or are they centred round our own personal schemas?

As **Anaïs Nin** famously said:

> # "We don't see the world as it is, we see it as we are."

Worth thinking about as you head on through this chapter.

It may be worth forgetting the complexity and ambiguity of the science and simply considering that any psychometric tool is simply a conversation starter – it allows individuals and teams to have safe conversations about how and why they operate the way that they do. Perhaps use them in parallel with the earlier team talk exercise.

It is a combination of many things that make a culture (environment, history, processes, policies, structure). People are the most important and influential aspect of a culture so with that in mind, here are some useful questions to ask regarding people:

1. **How will the team need to be set up to best deliver the purpose? What does that structure look like? Remember that too many levels equate to confusion and too many mixed agendas.**

2. **What are the roles and responsibilities? What do you need each person to be accountable for?**

3. **What skills, traits, attributes do you already have that you may just need to juggle around?**

4. **Do you really know who you are, how you like to operate in a team and how you come across to others?**

5. **What does each person need to be operating at their best? (Not just physical things like laptops/tablets, desks etc., but also consider the wider psychological things that people need – time and support for families, hobbies development opportunities etc.) What motivates them (and you)?**

6. **Which psychometric profiling tool(s) might help us?**

Let us talk about motivation
Can you motivate people to be committed to a vision?
What was your answer to that question? Most leaders say yes. The truth is that you cannot motivate people. I can now hear the collective intake of breath at a statement that surely is not correct. Let us look at why.

Firstly, what is motivation?
In its simplest form it is about two things – push and pull (also called extrinsic and intrinsic motivation).

Extrinsic motivation
This is when you use external factors to encourage people to do what you want. Extra pay, bonuses, time off and the threat of losing your job are all extrinsic motivators – some positive, some not.

Intrinsic motivation
This is internal. It is about having a personal drive to do something without being told to do so. Intrinsically motivated people are generally happy doing the job they do.

Every team member is different and will likely have different motivators. So, it is important to get to know your people, understand what motivates them so that they can be self-motivated. A one size fits all approach does not work.
You cannot tell people to be motivated, you can however, create the right environment and culture that taps into their own internal and personal motivators. Let us look at this another way.

Follow me, we are off to the garden.

How does your flower bed look?

A different way of looking at motivation and team performance.

As I write this spring has most definitely sprung here in the UK, which means I can get back into the garden again. This is one of my favourite places to be – there is nothing quite like spending the time and effort in preparing, sowing, and nurturing vegetable patches and flower beds (oh, and cutting the grass).

While I was pottering away in my borders last weekend my mind was idly wandering (as it tends to do) and I was thinking about some exciting team projects that I am currently designing for some amazing clients. One client, a big player in the manufacturing industry, has an issue with performance management – in particular, they are struggling to make it an even and fair process across the entire workforce. What the managers in this particular organisation tend to do is concentrate on those that are either performing really well (the easy option) or the ones who are under performing (the difficult conversation scenario). When looking at the underperformers (their words, not mine), they only concentrate on the things not being done as opposed to all the good things that are being delivered. This is a sign of bad leadership and a hindering team culture which will inevitably lead to a disengaged, inefficient, and demoralised workforce.

While looking at the various flowers now starting to come fully to life in my garden it got me thinking! What if we looked at our teams like a flower bed?

Bear with me now...

If you have a flower bed what does it look like? Does it have a few thrusting flowers that are standing out more than any others with beautiful colours shining through? Are some plants wilting or dying? Or perhaps your flower bed looks like a sanctuary for weeds – so overgrown you have forgotten what it was supposed to look like in the first place?

Every plant, flower, and shrub (and weed) needs certain things to thrive. For example, all plants need water, sun (some prefer more shade) and nutrition from the earth (or extra added goodness fed to them via a keen gardener).

As soon as you take away one of these elements the plant will wither and potentially die after a period of time. It is interesting (and at times frustrating for us gardeners) because all plants differ slightly (as I have spent years finding out to my cost), some love constant sun, some need soaking, others hardly any water (some succulents for example), some are extremely hardy and can be left on their own for long periods of time and others are an absolute favourite for slugs and snails.

My thinking continued as I pulled out weeds from around my Clematis – people are no different. Every human needs a set of core, basic essentials for life (oxygen, water, food etc.) and in order to not only survive but thrive, people need more. Just like plants – those needs are different for every individual.

Now transpose this across to your team and/or business – what does it look like? Are you feeding your thrusting flowers/plants (people) because they look good and seem to be performing well, whilst simultaneously ignoring the weeds in the hope that if you ignore them they will just die off in due course, even though currently they are draining goodness from the flower bed (your team)? What is causing the not so great looking flowers to wilt and your team flower bed to be uneven and ineffective? It could be your current team culture, your processes, your strategies, a lack of trust and truth in the team, not having a common team language, but here is the crux of it – the answer could be YOU.

I will let you digest that and really give it some thought.

Motivation should be an everyday event in business and not just part of a yearly appraisal. They do not work – it is the equivalent of doing the garden once in spring because the sun is out and then leaving it for the rest of the year.

Look to build a perennial team not an annual one
People need feeding every day, this means feedback, this means praise, this means reward and recognition and a million other motivating things that are different for every single human being. Do not simply choose to notice the things people are not doing (this could be your inability to communicate what you want clearly) – see the positives too.

If you are a leader then you are not only an architect (as I mentioned in my initial thoughts about leadership) you are also the gardener of your team – you should feed, nurture, inspire, enthuse, coach and help grow every individual in the team, in order for them to be the very best that they can be. You need to understand that everyone is human, and we all have individual motivators that, when tapped in to, make us a much more amazing part of a team. You cannot simply impose your shiny vision on people and expect them to be instantly motivated towards it.

Ask yourself a few questions.

1. **What would you like your flower bed to look like?**

2. **Have you lost track of what the original flower bed was supposed to look like?**

3. **Are you just feeding the weeds?**

4. **Do you know what makes your people grow and thrive?**

5. **Are you ignoring the tough conversations because it is easier to concentrate on the highflyers?**

6. **Are you letting external factors (slugs) effect the team?**

All effective teams need to be filled with people who are motivated. That is why it is vital that you keep tapping into the individual's motivators for each person within your team. You can encourage this process by creating an environment that helps them to become more intrinsically motivated.

An example

Fred (name changed) works for an organisation in the waste and environmental industry and has done for over 20 years. He works a set shift pattern from Monday to Friday. He does his job to the standards laid out in his job spec and contract of employment etc. and that is it. His (fairly new) manager wanted to push Fred a bit more and take him out of his comfort zone (to develop him) so started giving Fred some incentives (extra pay for more work for example). It became apparent quickly that this did not work. This had no motivational effect on Fred whatsoever. Why? Well clearly, he was not driven by money or financial reward.

Fred's manager had a coaching session with me and as a result decided that he would take a different approach. He went away and got to know Fred better. In a subtle way over a period of time he got to learn about Fred's family, his history and his hobbies. It was the final one that gave him the breakthrough – it transpired that Fred was a passionate football coach and that come rain or shine, he would get up early every Saturday to coach an under 11's football team (who were very successful in their local league). This is powerful to know! Why? Well it tells you several things about Fred.

* **He is self-motivated to get up on his day off to do something and not be paid for it.**
* **He loves to make a difference in a team environment.**
* **He likes to win.**
* **He is good at organising things (players, fixtures, transport etc.)**
* **He is a good communicator to the football team and the parents.**
* **He is exceptionally good at calming conflict (again with both the team and the parents).**
* **He has pride in what he does.**
* **He has many traits of great leadership.**

As a result of knowing this information Fred's manager decided to tap into this in order to get Fred to take on more responsibility within the team at work. He asked Fred for HELP. "Fred, I am struggling with the shift rotas at work and the handover meetings aren't working. I know that you are really good at this sort of thing with the football team so could you help me with it?"

Fred was happy to help [who does not like being asked for help because they are good at something?]. His skills [and more importantly, his intrinsic motivators] were being asked for and tapped into. From that point Fred took responsibility for the shift rotas and the format of the handover meetings. What happened?

Team shift handovers improved immensely; Fred was doing a little extra work [that he had not thought of before] because he wanted to.

All it took was for his manager to open his thinking a little, get to know his people and not assume he knows what makes them tick.

We make assumptions

Your leadership style is influenced by your beliefs. For example, do you think some people in your team are lazy or dislike working, and need continuous supervision or telling what to do? Or, do you believe that they are happy getting on with their jobs, and are likely to enjoy greater responsibility and freedom [like Fred]? These two fundamental beliefs form the backbone of the team motivation concept Theory known as X and Theory Y created by Douglas McGregor way back in the 1950s.

Theory X managers are authoritarian. They believe that their team members do not want or need responsibility, and that they have to motivate people extrinsically. Theory Y managers believe that their team members want more responsibility and should be part of the decision-making process [see chapter 4]. They assume that everyone has something valuable to offer.

The key thing here is to remember that the way we think affects the way that we act [actions and behaviours]. So, your beliefs about your team members' motivation affect the way you behave toward them. So, it is important to think carefully about how you view your people, and to explore what truly motivates them [intrinsically].

Personalise your approach

Remember, your team is made up of different individuals who have their own unique cultural norms, current circumstances, and past experiences. Consequently, each person may be driven by different motivating factors. When you make an effort to understand each and every team member, you can help them stay (self) motivated. Unlocking motivation in your team and encouraging them to exceed their expectations will help you to encourage loyalty, trust, and support and therefore a higher performing (and happier) team.

Remember push and pull. It is easier to pull someone towards something that they are intrinsically motivated to than to push your own ideas of motivation on them. I have mentioned the importance of the recruitment process several times. It is imperative that when you recruit people for your team you are open and honest about what the vision is and what values you operate by right from the off and ensure that this matches their own values and motivations as much as possible. If there is little match, then maybe the team is not for them. You will find that you are trying to force them to be motivated further down the line.

If you have recruited well and your team members are established, then the importance of continually developing them is vital.

Individual and team development

A word of warning here, be careful with the training and development providers that you select. Take the time to choose the right people to deliver the right development at the right time and for the right reasons.

Have you ever been on a training course or team building weekend and after a short space of time glazed over, become disengaged and realised that it has absolutely no relevance or cross over to your real life? It is always sad to hear about this happening to teams. It is sometimes after this has happened that we get approached at Successfactory™ for help.

Effective training and development requires stimulation of the senses and must be relevant to the person or team's real life. It must resonate and then achieve something real.

You do not necessarily need to use role play (not many people like this) to recreate or simulate real situations so that the team can connect the learning to real experiences, just make it relevant.

4. Tell me and I will forget, show me and I will remember, let me do it and I will understand. So true! Aid understanding by using sensory activities to illustrate or explore a theory or topic. Do not just talk about it – immerse people in it. Discuss a point and then show how this works in real life. Pushing people slightly out of their comfort zones helps here – activities like high ropes, problem solving, and team tasks are all good for cementing key theory points but only when used as part of the learning and not just a stand-alone bit of fun.

5. Follow up all training and development post event. Keep engaging with the team and challenge them if they are not applying the learning to their world. If it is not working, then change it.

Stimulating the senses in training shouldn't just be a gimmick just to make training more interesting or fun but it should be an integral part of the learning that reinforces key points and have crossover to the real world of the learners.

At Successfactory™ we pride ourselves on doing this very well.

Back to motivation

You probably spend a lot of your waking life at work (and maybe even some of your dreams are taken up by it too). Have you ever really stopped to think about why you do it and the impact it has on you and others?

I have created 20 extremely useful questions to ask yourself about your motivation! They have been compiled over many years of working with leaders and teams of all levels in many different businesses. They are frank, open, and impactful questions (if you choose to answer them 100% honestly). They may open your mind to areas of your working life that need improving.

Get yourself a coffee/tea/beer/wine or whatever you fancy, grab a notebook and pen and find a quiet and comfortable place where you feel relaxed. Turn off distractions and spend some quality time answering these questions.

Be honest!

1. **What motivates me to come into work every day and do the job that I do? It is important to stress that the question is NOT 'why do I go to work?' (most people say money) It is 'why do I do the job that I do?' (A subtle but significant difference).**

2. **Am I completely clear about what is expected of me at work? This is deeper than simply having a job role or job spec etc. Do you have discussions with your boss and peers about the job, what it entails right down to the subtle nuances?**

3. Do I have the correct and most up to date equipment/tools I need to do my job?

4. At work am I given the opportunity to do what I do best on a regular basis? (Does the team, including the boss, know what I am best at?)

5. Do I receive recognition or praise for excellent work? Or, do I simply get picked up for the things that do not go so well?

6. Does my boss care about me as a person?

7. Does my boss encourage my development?

8. Do I really know the people I work with?

9. Do I have a good friend at work? Or at least someone I feel I can talk to should I need a friendly shoulder to lean on.

10. Does the mission/ambition and vision of the company I spend many hours of my life working for make me feel like what I do is important and worthwhile?

11. Are the rest of my team committed to doing excellent quality work?

12. Do I talk to my boss and colleagues regularly about how I feel?

13. What more could I do to make my relationships at work better?

14. Do I have opportunities at work to learn and grow?

15. Do my boss and the business generally concentrate more on numbers/tasks or behaviours/people?

16. Do I and the team share best practice and best thinking with each other?

17. Does the team I am part of talk openly and honestly (even with difficult topics)?

18. At work, do my opinions seem to count? Am I listened to?

19. Do I have belief in myself? Do I have belief in the team? Do I have belief in the business?

20. Am I truly happy doing what I do?

How did you get on?
The questions should help you to realise if you know yourself and others in the team (including your boss) and if you are being authentic. It is important that every team member in a high performing team is authentic. If you are not being your true self and you are trying to change your behaviours to be something else this takes energy. Instead, use your authentic energy and you (and the team) will benefit massively.

Hopefully, you will have found some areas that you can now focus on to make your work life what you want it to be. If your answers to the questions do not sit well with you and things are not quite right - the good news is that you can do something about it! Remember that we all have a choice. We can change things that bother us, we can change our attitudes to the things that bother us, we can live with the things that bother us or we can escape the things that bother us.

It is your choice.

Summary – People

Teams only succeed through people. Not numbers, not equipment but people. The way you recruit and then treat your people is paramount to your long-term sustained success as a high performing team.

Never let the numbers, tasks or fancy corporate words hide that fact. The recruitment process needs to be deliberate and robust in who it selects to join a team. This starts with knowing what the team has been/is being set up to do – its purpose, and then establishing a strategy and a set of values that shapes the culture. Until this is done you cannot recruit members to the team.

Although they are important it is not just about skills and experience when choosing your people. For a team to succeed longer-term it is vital that you recruit the 'right fit' to your culture. You can train skill and gain experience, what you cannot do is change a person's deep-rooted personality – do not waste time and energy trying to.

Use personality profiling tools but do not get bogged down in them. Although some are better than others (in my opinion) they are all based in the same early theories of personality traits. They are a conversation starter. Use them as part of a recruitment process and then as a continuing learning and development guide within the team alongside other tools.

Remember that motivation for every team member will be different so tap into what motivates each other (which is why you must know each other well) and use these individual motivators to reach team success.

Create a perennial team that is robust and can sustain high performance, even under pressure.

> ## "But if thought corrupts language, language can also corrupt thought."
>
> George Orwell, 1984

This section is not about a specific language like English or French etc, it is more about the micro language that a team uses. This is a big part of a team's culture. Language is extremely powerful and should be used wisely.

If I had a pound [or dollar/euro etc., for our non-UK currency friends] for every time I had been asked for help to 'improve a team's communication', I would be decidedly better off than I am.

Communication is a massive topic, and just as with culture there are a wealth of reading materials readily available on the subject. I would however like to highlight a few points that I feel are relevant.

This is not a communication module – it is not going to delve into statistics about whether a certain percentage of communication is verbal versus body language [there are many differing views on this] or talk about how you can role play to learn to communicate 'better'. What it aims to do is highlight the importance of having a shared understanding of the micro-language you use and how you can communicate within the team in a way that works for you all.

In my experience I have found that most teams are good at understanding what they do and how they should do it (sometimes with a little help to get that clarity) but what they are not so good at is fully understanding the 'why'. I would like to introduce you to the why triangle – use this as a visual reminder to not forget the 'why' when creating your own strategies.

The WHY Triangle

Logic

WHAT

HOW

Teams are usually good at knowing 'what' they are doing

Teams are also pretty good at knowing 'how' they should do the things they do

Emotion

Emotion = MOTION

WHY

But many teams forget the importance of 'why' they are doing what they do

Do not simply concentrate on the what and the how – consider the why!

This should form the backbone of your purpose and vision.

Vision was mentioned a fair amount in chapter 1, and I used the analogy of a ladder that must be balanced. The picture below is a brilliant visual representation of this. It is taken from the amazing book, Strategies of the Serengeti© by Stephen Berry. I would highly recommend reading this book, in my opinion it is the best book I have ever read on strategy.

Steve and I worked together on a project in the Czech Republic a few years ago. We were working with the senior leadership team of a global manufacturing company who were very keen on developing their talent pool and having a robust succession plan for the leadership of the business. During a series of workshops, we talked about different ways of looking at recruitment and creating the desired culture that is both local but also aligns to the bigger picture [see chapter 1 of this book]. Steve and I used the ladder to open up discussion and debate about strategy and what the leadership role in strategy creation is. I have witnessed many organisations create a structure and then try and shoehorn a strategy into it. This is the wrong way round and rarely works effectively.

As Alfred Chandler once said,

"Structure follows strategy."

Build your purpose, your vision, and the foundations of your culture before you do anything else. Then link your Purpose/Mission, Vision, Objectives, Strategy, Tactics, Behaviours, and Values together. Once you have done this you can then fit the structure to suit it. Do not forget that this is a living process and the cycle will continue to change and adapt.

So, the whole picture looks like this:

Strategy Pyramid

| Activities/Actions |
| Tactics |
| Strategies |
| Objectives |
| Values |
| Culture |
| Vision |
| Purpose |

Continual Cycle

"We are re-evaluating
our strategy for the next
3-5 years and are struggling,
can you help?"

This is one of the top questions I get asked by clients at Successfactory™. The first thing that I ask them to do is send over their current strategy plan so that I can take a look and get a feel for it. It is pretty much always the same – I get sent a massive document that I struggle to remain engaged with after the first 3 pages.

I have observed many businesses create long-term strategy plans that are intricately complicated, covering every possible associated risk with a posh looking project plan, colourful Gantt charts, graphs and data and everyone having an abundance of enthusiasm. Then what happens? Reality is what happens, and the brilliant plan gets lost.

I am going to put this out there right from the off – 1, 3 or 5-year strategy plans do not work! There, I said it. I know there will be people who have just read this and thought about throwing the book across the room in contempt. 'How can you say that?' 'We have spent hours creating our long-term strategy – it is going to be an enormous success!'

What you have created is a dream, the overarching goal, the utopia. That is brilliant and important – think back to chapter 1 where we looked at the importance of having a compelling vision. What it is not is a robust strategy. Too much will change as soon as you start any project – as the well-known saying from the military states, "No plan survives contact with the enemy". You can spend hours planning for an operation only for everything to change the minute the boots hit the ground. Planning is important of course but it does not give all the answers. I would suggest that the process of planning is more important than the plan [more on this later]. How do you and the team react when you realise that the initial plan is not worth the paper it is written on?

"Things are always changing.
Part of being successful is being
comfortable not knowing what's
going to happen."

Susan Wojcicki, CEO of YouTube

What is more powerful (and successful) in the modern VUCA (Volatile, Uncertain, Changeable, Ambiguous) world we now operate in is the creation of shorter-term strategy plans. Keep the overarching vision (utopia) as a pin in the map to remind you of the destination but start creating short-term norms.

Short-term norms

Rather than having a huge overpowering and daunting 50-page document that says 'this is our vision and strategy for the next 3 years, start to break it down into small steps. This way you can create the required culture which is what I mean by norms.

Imagine that you are planning and leading a group on a walking route. You have a map and a compass, and you are keen to get going. Let us say that you are walking a 20-mile route and it finishes at a pub (as all good walks should). Would you simply look at where you intend to end up and then head off in that direction? Probably not the best plan. It would help if you were to create some way points along the route. Little tick offs that let you know you are still going in the right direction. Imagine that on this walk the weather closes in and your vision is limited by fog. If you do not have smaller, more achievable check points (strategies) then you are going to go off course very quickly. Having been part of several expeditions around the world I am very conscious of how easily this can happen, even with the most experienced navigators and mountain leaders.

This is about tactics – how you will deviate from a plan on the ground when necessary (but keeping the end goal in mind so that you can re-route back to it). This is the agility bit that is so vital to a plan.

An example of agility with a plan

A sub-team that I led in Afghanistan had the vital role of setting up communications from a newly established Forward Operating Base (FOB) in Southern Helmand Province back to the main joint force's HQ at Camp Bastion. We sat down together and planned our mission using the Combat Estimate 7 Questions framework.

1. **What is the situation and how does it affect me? What are the enemy doing and why?**

2. **What have I been told to do and why?**

3. **What effects do I need to achieve and what direction must I give to develop my plan?**

4. **Where can I best accomplish each action or effect?**

5. **What resources do I need to accomplish each action or effect?**

6. **When and where do the actions take place in relation to each other?**

7. **What control measures do I need to impose?**

We planned for the team to go in first to establish basic security and communications back to HQ and then the stores needing to establish more robust and long-term communications would be flown in by a separate helicopter once the ground was good.

What happened was the team arrived, set up initial communications and then maintained the security of the FOB whilst waiting for the additional stores to arrive. They did not. The priority for helicopters was a continuous (and often frustrating) juggling act for all involved and on this occasion we were not top of that priority list. What did my team do? Without any direction from me they simply changed the plan on the ground and adapted it to use what was available to them locally so that relatively stable communications could be maintained at least until further support was available.

They had little of the logistics that we had planned for but what they did have was the tenacity, innovation and resiliency to just get on with it.

The military are good at training people to deal with what they call dislocated expectations. Get used to things changing on the ground and ensure that your team has the right culture and mind-set to adapt your tactics accordingly.

Military mind-set in a civilian context

When the UK was in lockdown because of the Covid-19 pandemic I was asked to help a senior leadership team carry out 'crisis planning' more effectively during that rather chaotic situation. The team operated in the care sector and were therefore at the front of the virus challenge and did an amazing job! (They continue to do so I may add).

Using a mixture of military and business thinking I walked the team through the Mission Critical Planning cycle. My ideas were of course born out of my military experience where critical mission planning was crucial to success. I made it less military and more business-like by changing some of the wording but, it was based on the military method of rapid mission planning.

During critical times when quick planning and concise language are vital many teams make the mistake of trying to 'win the entire war' and become less effective at the smaller missions (battles) within the war. In business this equates to the smaller situational tasks that feed into the bigger picture of BAU (business as usual).

Here are the steps:

Clarify what the mission is

Establish clarity within the whole team as to what the top challenge/priority is. If this thing does not happen now, there is potentially catastrophic impact further down the line. Then turn this into a mission statement. Our mission is...in order to... [this covers the WHAT and the WHY]. It is vital that all team members fully understand the mission and that there is no ambiguity.

Controllables

Look at all aspects within this mission that are within your control. You cannot control some things [like the weather] but you can plan accordingly for different scenarios. Sometimes controllables are missed or mis-understood. It is easy during an after-action review [more on this later] to say, 'that was outside of our control'. In reality, some of the uncontrollables could have been spotted during the planning phase.

Capture Ideas

This is the start of the problem-solving part of the planning. Looking at individual weak points of the plan and capture ideas to reduce or negate them. Do not over analyse at this stage.

Take one individual challenge within the bigger challenge/mission at a time.

A great tool to help with this is Red Team Thinking.

This is an extremely useful tool where you look at your own plan from the enemies' perspective [Substitute 'enemy' with business competition, customer etc., as appropriate]. What are the weak points of the plan from the other side, i.e. where would you attack it if you were them? Cover every angle. Look at the mission statement and then look at every conceivable aspect that could go wrong – all the potential weak points of the plan and then concentrate on making those bits stronger and factoring in some contingency plans. Capture all ideas of how you can reinforce those weak parts of the plan – make them stronger and less risky.

Condense ideas

This is the first time that you analyse ideas. As a team, look at all the captured ideas from the previous stage and then clump together those that are the same or similar, so you end up with clear banks of ideas under different headings.

Clarify

Take the time at this stage to ensure that every team member understands each bank of ideas. Do not have any ambiguity as this will lead to plans potentially failing due to misunderstandings of the basics. Use a common language in the team. During time-critical planning you can condense any tool/process you normally use to be more tactical, agile and quick.

Counter Plan

This is where you start to add meat to the bones and the ideas become more detailed. You now start to link ideas together to form a strategic plan. You can start to use tools like Critical Timeline Right to Left, Left to Right planning to help you funnel down the plan to specifics.

To do this you will need time and space to think without distractions, so trying to do it when things are going mad around you is difficult.

Using a large white board or pin-board is advisable, but it can be done on flip charts or the floor/tabletop. Have some different colour pens to hand and start by writing down your end goal/mission on the right-hand side of a timeline. On the far left-hand side of that timeline write 'now' [see diagram]. Now, working backwards from your mission/goal think about everything that you need to do to achieve it [collective discussion]. Every conceivable thing! Write things on post-its so they can be moved around. Put them in an agreed order of priority. Working backwards to start with helps with this as you keep asking the question, 'in order to get here what must happen directly before it?'. This takes time and you will move post-its around [a lot]!

Once you have gone from right to left [i.e. you finished with the first thing that you need to do on the timeline after 'now'], go the other way from left to right and fill in any potential gaps. Keep asking the questions 'what else?' And 'what if?'. I will never forget an instructor I worked with at the Infantry Training Centre in Brecon who we called 'What if'. He would constantly ask this question in battle training scenarios. It works though. Continue to do this collectively as a team to utilise everyone's strengths, thoughts and abilities. Capture every idea.

Now, using a different colour do the same thing again [right-left and then left-right] with all the potential risks/hazards/blockers at each stage/phase. Perhaps use Red Team Thinking here.

This gives you a visual representation of your timeline which remains changeable [it is on Post-its]. It is also a great way to involve everyone in the team and create brilliant discussion.

Right to Left - Left to Right Planning

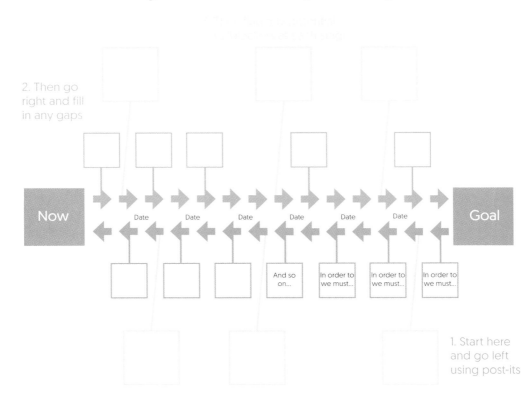

As part of your plan ensure that you have clearly defined and simple processes that can be conducted without the need for in-depth overthinking when the proverbial hits the fan. Make sure that you allocate roles and responsibilities so that it is clear to one and all what each person/team/sub team is going to do. This includes having a rota system of at least one person who keeps an eye on the 'war' – BAU bigger picture, as this may affect your mission.

Do

Put into action your plan(s) and carry out the mission. Actions not just words. Follow the plan but get used to dislocated expectations (no plan survives contact with the enemy) – as soon as the boots hit the ground, things will change. Be agile, learn as you go and adapt as needed to succeed in the mission. Ensure control is diluted to the lowest level.

After Action Review

Learn, Connect, Act

Use a review framework/tool/process to objectively look at what happened. What did you plan that worked well? What was planned but did not work? Why? What could have been done differently? Mistakes can be healthy – strive to learn. [More on this in chapter 5].

Celebrate Success

When you plan a goal think about how you will celebrate when you are successful. This is a powerful psychological tool as it switches the mindset of team members to the celebration and not the actual task/goal. In other words, the celebration becomes the goal.

Support Each Other

Always be ready to keep going. It is so vital that the team supports each other and factor in enough down time so that people do not burn out. You can only stay at peak performance for so long. Allow your body and mind to rest when possible.

Keep it as simple as possible

Do not try and win the war in one go – it will overwhelm you and the team. Concentrate on the success of each individual mission and overall success is much more likely.

Talking of overwhelming, I often see strategy plans that are far too complicated so I would like to introduce you to the idea of strategy planning on a page.

SOAP – Strategy on a page

SOAP recommended for all organisations and all business people to really clean up strategy planning.

When working with teams I challenge them to condense their strategy onto a page (I allow 2-sided). This strategy on a page can encompass your purpose, vision, mission, and strategies/actions. This forces you to cut away all the superfluous things that aren't needed and to have a clear, unambiguous and inspiring visual, on one page. There may of course be more information behind the one pager that adds weight, but it is the one page that people see and follow.

Here is an example of a process framework that I have used many times to create a plan on a page.

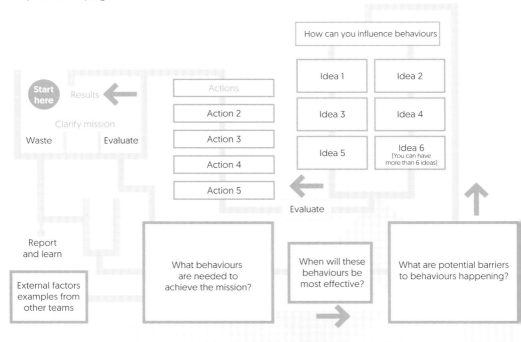

This looks quite complicated at first glance so let me take you through it.

The most important thing that came out of the first day of this team session was to stop and go back to basics. You may be the best weapon technician, the best chef on board a ship, have the best radar system etc., but if the ship does not float it really does not matter. Get the basic processes 100% right first and then build on them.

The basic processes that a team establishes should be engrained in the subconscious of every team member who uses them. They should be jointly developed, mapped out, vigorously tested, constantly challenged, and evaluated, and very importantly, consistently applied.

Processes should be simple enough that they become part of the team's unconscious competence.

Unconscious competence was a phrase first coined by Martin. M. Broadwell in 1969 and is when a person does something on 'auto pilot'. They are so practiced at it that it becomes second nature and requires no conscious thought. A great example of this is driving. If you do drive regularly to one location, let us say your place of work, how often have you arrived at that destination and have no real idea of the journey you have just taken? How many times did you change gear, indicate or brake etc? You do not know because you are operating on 'auto pilot'. Go back to when you learnt to drive. Things were a bit different then – to start with you had to concentrate on every detail of driving and your senses were fully alert and firing. Once you had been taught the basics of driving you became 'consciously competent'. In other words, you could do it, but you had to consciously think about it. As time goes by you become more experienced (and usually more confident) and you move more towards unconscious competence.

It is worth noting that it is very possible to move backwards on this scale. For example, if you have had an accident in the car you are likely to become much more conscious of your actions again or if you go to another country where they drive on the opposite side of the road to what you are used to then you will revert to conscious competence. You must consciously think.

It is useful to be aware of this concept because it can be helpful and hindering. Unconscious competence is great for speed but can also lead to lack of agility with processes. You literally just 'do' without stopping to think.

A good example from my own experience was when I trained to be a platoon weapons instructor. Learning to use various weapon systems in the military is a vital skill. Training would start off gently, understanding the weapon's capabilities, knowing the working parts and how they operate together, how to strip the various weapon systems down, cleaning and maintaining them and then the intricate process of effectively using them for their intended purpose by firstly firing in a controlled environment using the proven process of the marksmanship principles. This starts on a static range and progresses to live firing exercises under realistic real-life conflict simulated conditions.

When you analyse this the drills used are simply a set of simple, smaller processes that allowed us to use the weapons without even having to really think about it too much. In other words, the processes took the operating of the weapons from a conscious competence to an unconscious competence. It became intuitive – when the weapons jammed or stopped working properly you simply went through the drills (processes) that you had learnt to get back into the fight as quickly as possible. This is of course vitally important in operational situations as your mates are depending on you.

Everyone who used the weapons had received the same training using the same processes and as a result we were all confident in each other's ability to stay in the fight. Simply put – we had mutual trust in everyone's ability.

This is not to say that on the ground, when the proverbial was hitting the fan, decisions could not be made that deviated slightly from the processes. An empty rifle magazine would not get stowed away correctly in an ammo pouch; it would get thrown down the front of a smock for example. This is not what was taught but is a simple example of agility with a process that allowed the team to continue to move forward without delay. Speed was usually of the essence.

Here are some ideas to help with meetings that have been created by the Successfactory™ team after years of crafting and delivering hundreds of workshops and meetings in many diverse cultures and settings.

1. When planning a meeting the starting point must be the question, **what is the purpose of the meeting?** Always have a purpose to a meeting that is aligned to the team's goals and values. Sell the purpose of the meeting before people get there - they should want to be there and arrive curious, excited, and valued. If there is no purpose, then do not have a meeting.

"There is nothing so useless as doing efficiently that which should not be done at all."

Peter F. Drucker

2. Second question is, **what do you want people to do after the meeting?** The reason for having a meeting aside from the social interaction and team check-in is to create action. Chapter 5 looks at the concept of actions and not just words. If you have an idea of what you want to happen because of a meeting, then it can help shape that meeting and make it more focused.

3. Next, think about **how you want people to feel?** This is important as you need to create the right environment that means people feel comfortable both physically and mentally. What can you do to make people leave the meeting happy and inspired?

4. Fourth question is, **how are you going to inspire action?** As mentioned in point 2, action is one of the key objectives of a meeting. Rather than just tell people what they are going to do, how can you inspire them to want to do it?

5. **Invite individuals personally** to meetings and sell the value of them being there – the 'why' they need to be there. Inclusion equals commitment.

6. When working out who should be there ask two questions – **will they add value, or will they receive value?** If not, do not invite them.

7. **Never have AOB** [any other business]. Do the extra leg work needed before any meeting so that it is focused and any issues/challenges/questions are added to an agenda in advance of the meeting so that people can give it considered thought and come to the meeting prepared and armed with potential solutions/questions rather than suddenly being put on the spot at the end of a meeting. AOB is usually an excuse for people to just have a moan. This takes a meeting off track so avoid.

8. **Handle any negativity** at the start to give you time to raise desire and motivation so people leave on a high. If you do enough pre-work and follow the points here, then there should be no [or minimal] negativity.

9. When developing an agenda, you must develop **'the what' AND 'the how'** – use the best tools and techniques to tackle each item. It is helpful to write potential agenda points as a statement. In order to do xxx, we must xxx.

   So, as an example, "in order to complete this customer's order on time we must change the process line set up to work 24 hours rather than the current 18 hours." Then write each agenda topic as a **question** to get people in the right frame and to get them thinking about solutions.

   So, to change the example above into a question would look something like this – 'Agenda point 1 – How can we possibly change the process line set up to work 24 hours rather than the current 18 hours?' Send the agenda out to everyone in **advance** of the meeting so they have time to look at the questions and formulate some ideas before turning up.

10. During a meeting make it a team 'norm' that no one asks, "Do you understand?" Instead, ensure that you **check for clarity** using questions and further dialogue. Challenge people to verbalise what they are going to do (actions). I have personally witnessed people leaving a meeting having said they are happy and understand what needs to be done only to have a separate conversation with a colleague in the corridor asking, "what was that all about? What do I actually need to do?"

11. **Use technology appropriately** but do not overuse it or rely on it. Plan a meeting with the thought, what happens if all the technology goes down? Rather than putting up endless charts, graphs and PowerPoint slides find diverse ways of displaying things. I was once working with a finance team that used people from the team who stood up at different heights holding number cards to illustrate the financials rather than put them on a boring graph on the screen. They created a human graph. People were engaged and they remembered it. Brilliant!

12. Remember that **there are never difficult people at meetings**. As St Francis of Assisi said, "seek first to understand". 99% of work interaction has good intent – what is their intent?

    Think of someone you know who you deem to be a difficult person (in your opinion) and now think what you are telling yourself about your next encounter with that person. If you are being completely honest then you are probably telling yourself that future interactions with this person will also be difficult. Your mind has learned a set way of thinking regarding experiences with this 'difficult' person and defaults to this (negative) thinking for each time you interact with them.

    Because your mind is expecting a difficult experience, it interprets the encounter as difficult. This may not be a 100% accurate account of the event but simply what you have convinced yourself of as fact. Do not forget that everybody has their own programmes for different situations (including encounters with you).

If you are encountering difficulty with people in meetings, consider also that you may be using the wrong processes and/or language or that you simply have the wrong people in the meeting. If a person is being deliberately belligerent and disruptive there will be a reason for this.   Extract them from the meeting (nicely) and at a convenient time (ideally when you have just finished the meeting) iron this out while it is fresh. Talk to them and learn why. It is important to do this away from the meeting and it is important to leave emotion out of it. If it transpires that the issue is a wider team one, then invite the individual back to the meetings in future and use tools to tackle the problem/challenge.

Also, try changing the language you use. Delete 'difficult' and insert 'interesting'. Language is powerful, use it wisely.

13. Actions should leave with everyone immediately. **Writing up actions days later is poor discipline.** You want action as soon as possible with complete clarity of what those actions are before people leave the meeting. This helps if you have a common team language.

14. Do not forget that you can use **different processes for different meetings**. Whatever process you use, make it fun, keep active, use nature, if you hold the correct PPL / PRS licencing, use music, keep it interactive, use visual facilitation, inspire action. Would you rather hear, "what was the point of that meeting? A complete waste of time and I am already snowed under" or "that meeting was great, really productive. I know what I need to do and what the team are doing, and why – I am looking forward to the next meeting". Some of the best meetings that I have been in have been 'walk and talk' – go for a walk and let the conversation flow.

15. Always look for ways to improve your meetings – **review and learn** every time.

There is quite a lot to think about there. I run sessions over several days with teams to really get into the depths of running meetings. The aim here is to get you thinking. Remember, get the basics 100% right first. Give some thought to whether your meetings currently follow the ideas above. If not, give them a go and see the difference it makes. If they are radically different to your current ways of doing things, then introduce them gently.

The same level of detail needs to be afforded to all the team's processes. It can be a timely task creating effective basic processes that work for the team. Do not think that this is time wasted – it pays off in the end.

Aside from meetings (above), here are some other processes that teams should consider. The list is not exhaustive – add your own that are relative to your purpose and situation.

Processes to consider:

- **Decision making**

- **Communicating internally and externally**

- **Various reporting processes**

- **Review and evaluation process. Learning from mistakes (more on this in chapter 5)**

- **Cross cover of all team tasks. If one member is not available how will the team and task continue as BAU. The customer should not see any difference to the team's output**

- **Changing task direction – think back to the idea of 'traffic'. Does your team culture create autonomy or control? Is agility centrally governed or controlled on the ground by individuals closest to the task output? How does this change in direction happen in the team?**

- **Information storage and sharing processes**

- **Your procurement processes**

- **Training, learning and development processes**

- **Succession planning**

- **Basic HR (people) processes**

- **Marketing and PR. Dealing with media**

- **The process of risk assessment and risk reduction**

- **Setting up specialist project teams**

- **Strategy planning**

Again, a lot to think about but nobody said this high performing team stuff was always easy!

A top tip is to keep your processes as simple as possible. If you do not, then people will not follow them – they will find their own way. It is human nature to find the path of least resistance.

Simplify the complex.

Some final questions about processes to consider:

1. **Are your team processes the simplest that they need to be to get the job done?**

2. **Are your processes mapped out in an easily understandable format?**

3. **Do people follow the processes?**

4. **Do you create processes together as a team? If not, why not?**

5. **Are your processes fit for purpose but agile and does every team member have them engrained in their subconscious?**

6. **How do you evaluate and adapt your processes?**

Summary – Processes

Processes are the cement that hold the bricks of a team together. They are vital, so rather than fighting against them, make them work for you. Perhaps look at it as if you are creating useful habits that will help the team achieve success. To create effective processes the team must have an inclusive and adaptive culture and it must use past and present knowledge wisely.

Processes are the check points that keep you on track and allow everyone in a team to understand a common way of doing things. The basic processes of a team should never be over-complicated and should be part of each members' subconscious. However, processes also need to be continually tested and evaluated to check that they remain fit for purpose. If they are not, then adapt them. If you do not do this, then people will quickly lose trust in them and the team's ability to operate effectively.

CHAPTER 3. TRUTH & TRUST

● Truth ALWAYS

● Have trust in each other and in what happens when things don't go to plan

"Integrity is telling
myself the truth.
And honesty is telling
the truth to other people."

Spencer Johnson

If you cannot tell the truth and be open and honest with
each other then you may as well stop now! But that is a little
defeatist, so perhaps instead of giving up, let us look at ways
to create a culture where it is ok to tell the truth to each other.

If you do not have a culture of trust in your team then you
will struggle to tell the truth to each other. Telling the truth
should be on every team's charter — something that is a non-
negotiable. So just take a moment to consider if the trust is in
place. If not, then start there and come back to this chapter.

"Truth is the crossroads of perspective."

Stewart Stafford

I have found that usually it is when opinions are used that the truth gets blurred and creates problems. You know what they say about opinions. An opinion is not necessarily the truth or fact and is likely to elicit an emotional response in an individual or a team.

So, when speaking the truth to members of the team use facts. Unless someone is being deliberately obtrusive or belligerent then they cannot argue with facts.

What is it that makes telling the truth difficult? There are many reasons, and everyone is different of course. On many occasions it is the fear of both the initial reaction and then the longer-term consequences that stop us saying it as it really is. Add to this the fact that humans like to be liked. This is a trait that we all possess to varying degrees. The idea of someone not liking us does not sit well with our psychology as we like to feel part of the group. I believe social media has compounded this. In a world where a thumbs up and a like is seen as a 'must have' people have become even more obsessed with being 'liked'. The other thing about social media is that it is quite easy to sit behind a screen and say what you like but how many times have you seen a keyboard warrior rant about an 'issue' only to be as quiet as a mouse when confronted about it face to face. Telling the truth and discussing/debating a point is harder to do when you are face to face because you have real-time reactions. There is also the fear of course that the other person or people could retaliate in both a verbal and physical way in some instances. If anything, social media has made us less sociable (in my opinion).

Conversely, some people have absolutely no hesitation in calling it out like it is no matter what the consequence or impact is. This is also not a great approach as it can cause resentment, misunderstanding and a breakdown of effective team communication.

There needs to be a middle ground, one where people's sensitivities are considered, and thought is given to the consequences of things that are said. This is, in part, the way that things are said and how the other person or people receive what is said. Mind-set and culture play a big part in this which is why in order to be able to tell the truth, an open, honest and safe culture must first be built.

The ideal is to have a level of emotional intelligence that means you take into account other people's feelings and weigh them up with the need to talk openly and honestly and get to the point. Say it as it is but with the perspective of the other person/people in mind.

There are many occasions when not being open and honest has led to the downfall of a team/business or organisation. You only need to look at politics to see this happen on a daily basis. The media are also guilty of this.

On the flip side, there are many examples of when telling the truth has really paid off.

With this in mind, here are 8 questions for you to consider. Perhaps ask each member of the team to answer them first and then get together (maybe over a drink of choice) and discuss them as a whole team.

1. **Why is telling the truth in your team sometimes hard to do?**

2. **Think about an individual or organisation you know who did not tell the truth. What consequences were there?**

3. **What are the things that you see on a regular basis within your team/business that are wrong and could be put right if people were honest in confronting it?**

4. What are the implications/long-term impact of not talking about the elephant in the room?

5. Can you give examples where the truth has improved working relationships?

6. How could you make the truth easier to tell in your team? Is your culture one that freely allows the truth to be aired and received well?

7. What processes do you have in place to fact check and ensure legitimacy of the truth?

8. **Are you being authentic?**

Take some time to think about people that you have known or know now who are authentic in a positive way.

Ask:

1. What behaviours do you observe in them?

2. What language do they use?

3. How do they consider other people's thoughts and feelings when telling the truth?

4. How do people react to them?

5. How can you be more like that?

TRUST

"I'm not upset that you lied to me, I'm upset that from now on I can't believe you."

Friedrich Nietzsche

Trust does not come from a title or position. Trust is earned. If your team do not trust each other then it is vital to understand why.

There needs to be trust in each other and trust in what happens when things do not go to plan. As I have mentioned previously – there are many pitfalls of long-term planning. Having a plan is great – it gives you that warm comforting feeling that things are going to be just fine. The reality is quite different in many situations. Having trust in all team members when things do not happen as planned is imperative.

If you take a high performing sports team as an example – let's say a top-level rugby team (choose your own) you will often observe what great teams, with great leadership, do when things aren't going well. It is fascinating to watch. Firstly, when the ball is dropped/lost each player knows what to do in order to get into a defensive position and then ideally back into an attacking position as quickly as possible. Possession is key. This is about having the right processes that are engrained in people's subconscious and the right culture and mind-set with the addition of another important ingredient – trust in others to follow those processes.

When you measure your team's outputs do you measure things like trust? Do you have a KPI for it? If not, why not?

It can make life infinitely easier to have a process in place for decision making. It gives you a framework and guideline. That is not to say that you should not encourage a culture of free thinking, with open and honest critique of ideas, but that you should maybe have a few signposts that keep thinking on track.

This is more important if you are under time pressure and things need to happen quickly. It is under these pressure situations that having a process in place can really help.

I have always found that making decisions flounders when emotion is allowed to drive the process. This is not to say that emotion is not important as it usually allows people's true feelings to come to the surface and therefore, out in the open to be talked about.

How would you describe emotion? What is it?

What is emotion?

Emotion is not only a left-over trait from evolution, it is also constructed to communicate in social situations – it becomes situated in knowledge and is culturally and historically based. There are many theories that see emotion as a product of social rules and parameters which in turn lead to social and contextual expectations – in other words, the society we live in shapes our emotions. There are other theories that believe it is emotions within an individual that affect society's expectations of behaviour – it is the individuals' emotions that shape society. If this is the case, in a team context emotions are both shaped by and in turn shape the culture (the importance of which was discussed in chapter 1).

Many people believe that emotion is driven by chemical reactions in the body, but is it possible to reduce the explanation of emotion down to simple chemical reactions within the brain (as some biological psychologists will have you believe) or is there much more to the story? There appear to be set roles for both social and biological input to the production of emotion.

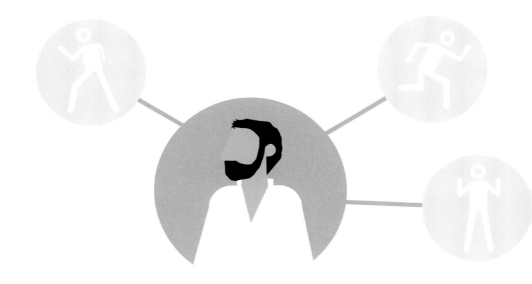

Basic emotions, such as fear, hold obvious evolutionary advantages – the chemical reaction and subsequent action (the fight, flight, or freeze response) can, quite literally save our lives. This is probably a fair assumption, but it does not explain more complex emotions which at first glance have little survival advantage to us, for example happiness, which can only really be regarded as a social signal to others. Therefore, it can be argued that some emotions go beyond the basic set needed for survival and are created by the social world in which we live.

Some emotions may even lead us to gravitate towards others who share similar traits and behaviours. This adds weight to the idea that we perceive events as relevant not necessarily to the reality but to things that we want or do not want, like or do not like. In other words, we shape our own reality by aligning it to what we want, which has been shaped over time and experience living in our own social and cultural norms. This seems like common sense – when do we not try to orientate to what we like?

It could be argued that the Machiavellian nature of humans could use emotion to our advantage to get what we want in certain situations and on the flip side, emotion has other functional uses like deflection away from ourselves. Neither of these things are healthy in a high performing team environment so it is important to be aware of them.

I also believe that there is a tendency for human beings to gauge our own emotion, relative to the reaction of others. So, we may have an inbuilt set of beliefs that drive our emotions and behaviours, but they can be manipulated by the social environment that we operate in. I call this the 'yawn effect'.

You have probably seen this happen – one or two people get emotional and others follow. A great example of this was 'Beatlemania' in the 1960s, where crowds of fans got swept along by mass group emotion. One could argue that this manipulation of an individual's emotions can lead to group think – a well know phenomenon that reduces a group's ability to make rational and unbiased decisions.

So, when it comes to decision making in a high performing team there needs to be a high level of objectivity. This will flex depending on the circumstances of course, human beings are emotional animals and some emotion will always be present. Individuals and the team should aim to base their decision making on FACTS. If you start a conversation with "I think" then instantly that becomes subjective. Start with what you know to be true at that time.

If you are in a highly emotional state then, if the situation allows, step away and return when things are more settled. There are numerous breathing exercises that can help when you feel emotional. Sometimes it is as simple as stopping and taking a breath.

Vocalised thoughts and opinions can be useful, as I said, they are manifestations of people's thoughts and feelings brought to the surface to be shared with the team, but they are also quite diverse and as I mentioned, are often based on an individual's cultural and social norms. The aim is to strive for objectivity when it comes to decision making.

It is always useful to have some tools in your team toolbox that help you make decisions. The bottom line is that it is always discussions that leads to decisions being made so you must be able to talk openly and honestly and be able to accept the facts when they are presented rather than fight against them.

A useful tool/process that can help the team with decision making is
Satellite Solutioning.

Firstly, ensure that the entire team are present and there are no other distractions [I appreciate that this can be difficult]. You will need several flip charts as a minimum but ideally, a couple of large white boards or large pin boards with plain paper attached. An open space with no [or limited] tables works best for this.

Here are the steps:

1. As a team discuss the following question – what is the issue you are tackling? You all need to be clear on this. You are then creating a statement. For example, 'we struggle as a team to communicate effectively across all our sites'.

2. Ask each team member to individually turn the statement into a question. For example, 'how could we possibly change the way that we communicate across our sites to make us more effective?'

3. Agree as a team what the question should be [amalgamate ideas and compromise here folks].

4. One person can write the agreed question up in the middle of a large white board or pin board paper.

It is important for the next stage that you have a dedicated timekeeper so that you do not spend too long over thinking. The one danger of this tool is that if it is not controlled well enough it simply ends up as a free for all with little clarity.

1. Now ask every team member to spend 10 minutes brainstorming ideas (on their own). Each person should jot down their own thoughts and ideas about how they would answer the question. Ensure that everyone uses the full time. Do not simply write a couple of ideas down and stop. Continue to challenge thinking by asking – what else? And, if that last idea didn't work, what else could we possibly do?

2. Once this is done, again, with one person scribing, spend some time (I would suggest 5-10 minutes depending on team size) capturing everyone's ideas on the large board. Do not talk over each other and do not analyse anything at this stage – simply capture. Do this by writing each idea around the centre question (like satellites around the earth).

3. Once all ideas have been written up give the team time to look at everything and digest it all.

4. Now, take one of the ideas/answers to the question and focus on only that one. Ask the question, 'what would stop this happening?' or 'what are the blockers?' Again, allow a period for the team to individually capture their own ideas to this question (I would allow up to 10 minutes). Timekeeper be strict on the time. The aim is to get people to think relatively quickly and capture what comes into their heads.

The next part is about capturing the potential blockers (to the one area of focus). The scribe should change colour of pen for this so that it is easy to see what an answer to the initial question is in the middle and what is a potential blocker.

Give the team time again to look at everything that has been captured, consolidate their thoughts and add/change things where necessary. It is important to not rush through this bit. Clarity of meaning is vital.

1. Now take one of the blockers. Again, ensure that there is clarity on what the words mean and that everyone agrees that this could potentially be a blocker, then ask the question, 'what can we do to reduce or eradicate this risk?'

2. Capture ideas for the first blocker of the first potential solution to the initial question written in the middle of the board. Concentrate only on the first blocker – if you try and do more than one at a time, things may get lost.

3. Now take the next blocker to the first potential solution and do the same thing again.

Once you have completed this for all the potential blockers to the first solution, move onto the next solution and repeat the process.

Once all solutions and blockers have been completed you can then turn the words into actions. Again, it is vital that everyone in the team agrees on the wording and meaning of each action.

Turn the ideas into actions on a visible action plan (second large board or flipcharts). A top tip is to not have too many actions. Keep it concise and keep it as simple as possible. I have experienced teams on many occasions trying to create action plans that are far too big. The more things on the list, the less that gets done.

Agree actions and accountability. Remember that actions are visible, repeatable, and measurable. Saying things like, 'we will communicate better' means nothing, it is not an action, it is a dream.

Accountability instils trust in a team, fosters courage to take appropriate risk, and empowers people to find solutions - even to the most daunting challenges.

Create an action plan/tactics in a format that works for you as a team (project plan, team charter, team canvas, ops list etc.)

Do the thing you have planned and then evaluate and go again as necessary.

As a member of a team your actions define you and impact the mood and behaviour of others. Really think about that! When you throw a pebble in a pond it is the ripples that flow outward that have the lasting effect. What differentiates a team from a high performing team is the ability to understand the wider impacts of behaviour and act accordingly.

It reminds me of the saying that I mentioned earlier in this book, 'the way the boss comes in in the morning is the way people will go home at night'.
What about you? Have you ever been in the situation where you have simply blurted out how you really feel to someone and it has backfired? I am guessing that we have all had a time where our mouths started before our brains fully engaged. We did not really mean some of what we said and in hindsight, we would have approached the situation very differently.

I would like to share with you a simple tool that helps to combat this happening – it is called AKAS. This simple framework can be used to review performance, tackle difficult behaviour, help resolve conflict, engage people with change and problem solving. This works even when you are working as a virtual team – before you have that online meeting or send that email – try this out.

Firstly, think about your issue/challenge and download your thoughts onto a piece of paper. Write it down exactly as you would blurt it out without thinking. This is for your eyes only, so be honest – what you would you really like to say? – Do this with absolutely NO FILTER.

Next, think about how many issues/challenges are involved in what you are thinking and feeling. Are all the separate issues/challenges linked and do they need to be looked at together? Do you need to break it down and tackle one thing at a time? How much of this issue is because of you? How much is within your control? Be honest here – park the ego!

Now stop writing. Go and do something else that takes your mind away from this completely. Take as much time as you can away from it.

When you come back to it, read through what you have written down and see what you feel/think about it now.

Now we delve into the AKAS bit...What I will say in reality...

Actual Problem – Description of the problem/opportunity. This is about using facts to engage people and avoid resistance, so how will you describe the problem/opportunity in a non-threatening, positive and engaging way? It is vital that you move from feelings to facts.

Knowledge – What do you know to be true? Use examples to make what you are talking about clear and un-ambiguous. Use actual data (not opinion), real evidence and information to clarify what you are saying. This helps to remove the emotion. It is also a good opportunity to convey how this issue has affected others – what has been the impact? (Use facts).

Ask Questions – This leads to engagement. What questions can you ask to involve and engage them with what you are saying? Think back to the four thinking components and how important questions are for shaping how people see their imagined future.

Solution Building – This is an open discussion. It is important at this stage to have effective dialogue about building a solution together. Be careful not just to deliver a solution that you have thought up yourself without consulting others in the team. Remember, inclusion equals commitment.

That's it! How simple is that?

Remember that we all have moments when emotions threaten to take over. Give yourself time to stop and consider the impact it will have on the team (and wider). Your actions and words define you and they can be enormously powerful.
So now that we have established the need for action and not just words, it is important to have a process in place to measure those actions.
How will the team measure its OUTPUTS?

As part of the process of building a team it is important to consider what the key performance measures will be in line with the overarching purpose. This should tie in with the individual roles and responsibilities that hold people accountable. Performance measures should be a mix of qualitative and quantitative data.

Here are some useful questions when looking at the performance requirements of the team:

1. How will you know you are successful?

2. What does success feel like for your team?

3. What are the key success factors? (The smaller things that need to be in place and ultimately lead to the overall success).

4. Do you celebrate success? If so, how?

5. Do you have KPIs? If so, are they the right ones? Could you call them something else?

6. How will you deal with not achieving performance?

7. Have you considered all external contributing factors that could impact your ability as a team to deliver?

8. What other performance measures are important to the team aside from the numbers? (What about happiness, fun and morale? Can they be measured?)

9. What language do we use to describe our performance?

Your actions should match your language. Language connects directly to the culture in a team (as does pretty much everything). It is worth noting that a conversation is a negotiation – we start with our own interpretative repertoires, our schemas and ideas about how things are and how they should be but these ideas are fluid and adaptable to change according to the social and cultural context at the time – our ideas are extracted from experience but that doesn't mean that our future has to remain the same as the past (remember the four thinking components?)

When planning and then subsequently measuring actions, it can be a good idea to do a high-level capture of the potential impact. I would like to share with you an example of a simple template that I often use with teams I am helping to develop. You can change the dates to suit what it is you are measuring. Plan using the template and when you review you can analyse whether you have achieved that impact.

Business Impact

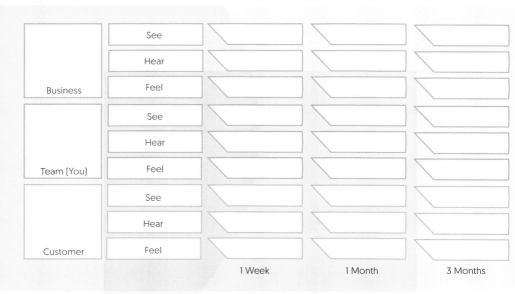

		1 Week	1 Month	3 Months
Business	See			
	Hear			
	Feel			
Team (You)	See			
	Hear			
	Feel			
Customer	See			
	Hear			
	Feel			

This is a great visual planning and review tool that uses both quantitative and qualitative measures to create discussion in the team. You can of course create your own tools and templates but just ensure you have some processes and tools in place to review actions effectively.

Think about a classic reporting structure in an organisation. It tends to look a bit like this?

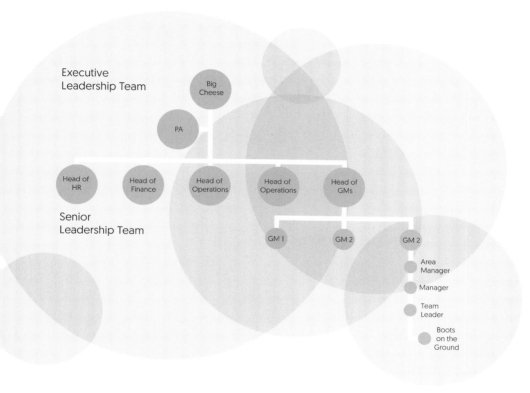

The problem with this structure is that issues and mistakes can be hidden. When a report is written from the ground – where the action is, it then goes up to the next level, let's say a team leader, who looks at the report and maybe tweaks it a little to hide some mistakes or failure to meet deadlines or whatever, in other words, it gets changed to make them and the team at that level look better. Now, the team leader passes this up the chain of command to their manager. What does that person potentially do? Yep, you guessed it – the same thing. The report gets tweaked and sent up to the next level and so on. Eventually the report will get to the top of the chain and the big cheese will possibly think everything is going swimmingly as all the reports ending up on their desk look good. Targets being met, people are happy, and processes are running as planned. Nice one!

Two lessons from this are that if your organisation has too many levels of leadership it dilutes your ability to communicate effectively from bottom to top and all ways in between and generally speaking the reports that reach the top do not reflect the reality on the ground. Watch out for this.

In the military (particularly in an operational theatre) this tends to not happen – the reality on the ground is all that matters. Good, bad, or indifferent the truth must be spoken. Bad news early and deal with it.

Even going back to my early military training, there were examples of good and bad leadership in terms of mistakes that were made. As a naïve young man, I was desperately trying to pick up what I was being taught and then put it into practice. Naturally, I made mistakes but the thing I remember is the reaction of the people training me. Most jumped on me (and others) straight away, shouted at us and 'beasted' us for not getting it right. This created a culture of fear so I did everything I could to hide any mistake I made. Not good!

There was however one of the instructors who was a little different. He listened and then asked further questions that dug down below the surface to the reality – the truth of why a mistake was made. He then coached (not the language that was used back then) me/us to do better next time and to succeed. This is true leadership.

Does your team have a coaching culture towards mistakes, or does it jump on people and create fear?

Coaching is about asking questions, and this is a vital part of a review process. I use a simple model with teams. It is called Do, Review and Understand. The brilliance of this is its simplicity. Many teams I help simply need to stop over complicating things and just apply.

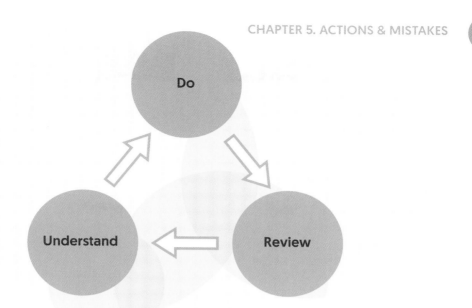

When reviewing it is a great idea to follow a format. It does not have to be rigid but simply an aid to keep you on track with a balanced view [both objective and subjective]. An example would be to look at the results that the team achieved during a task. To start with you are looking at the visible things that are measurable. The heading could be outcomes, statistics/numbers, and activities for example. As individuals answer the questions:

What went well? What could have been better?

That [in my opinion] is the easy part.

Now go below the surface and answer the same questions [what went well and what could have been better?] under the following headings:
methods, behaviours, and feelings.

Come back together as a collective team and analyse your thoughts.

1. **Do you agree on what went well and what did not?**

2. **What impact did individual behaviours have on the task?**

3. **What made people feel the way they did?**

Do not negate the feelings part because you think it might be a little too 'fluffy'. If you do think this is 'fluffy' then try sitting in with a military or sports team that does this and see what you think then. The way that people feel directly influences how they act and therefore has a big impact on team success.

An easy and colourful way to capture feelings is to use a feelings graph.

Here is an example of a team's feelings graph.

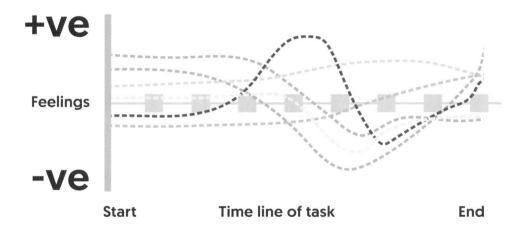

Ask individuals to map how they felt throughout the timeline of the task or project with a colour pen (it is best to do this on a large white board or flip chart). If you do not have different colours available, then ask everyone to initial their own lines.

Once everyone has done this, collectively analyse the 'why'. Where are the similarities? Do the lines match? Why were feelings low or high at that point? If the feelings were low, then what could you do differently to change that happening again in the future? Did feelings lead to mistakes. Do not forget to capitalise on the positives too – when were feelings high and how can you replicate that in the future?

Once all the areas of your review tool have been discussed you can consider and reach agreement on what should be stopped, started, and continued.

The team's job was to set up initial security, communications, and infrastructure ready to accommodate the first potential wave of refugees from across the mountains. I along with my boss, Bruce, were the first people from the battle group to set foot in the area. We stood in a large field overlooked by mountains in the distance, with the odd ramshackle old farm building just about standing but aside from that it was pretty barren and an incredibly beautiful and serene place. We set up an antenna system and established communications with HQ and made a brew. The rest of the team started to arrive over the course of the day.

We did not expect what happened next!

Within the course of only a few hours thousands of people descended into the area from across the border looking for safety and escape – we were overwhelmed and had to create more robust security very quickly in order not to be overrun. We did not crumble, we did not moan – we simply got on with it. Tents were erected [LOTS of tents], toilet areas built, supplies ordered in and plans put in place to establish and sustain the camp for an indefinite period. It was an amazing thing to witness and be part of. We were under immense pressure to get this place set up – people's lives depended on it. We had little sleep, and very tight time frames to work to, but it was under this stress that I saw some amazing things happen and some people, who were generally quiet and reserved, really come out of themselves and step up to the challenge. The pride created from this operation was immense. As a unit we talked about this for years after [mostly just amongst ourselves] and it remained an extremely proud success for us all. I mention this because pride is so important in a high performing team.

This is a process that a team should use in its working practices and not just on a ropes course – it is all about mentoring and supporting each other.

The top challenges of dealing with conflict that I am asked to help with most regularly are:

1. **People are not aware of the triggers of conflict in their teams.**

2. **An unwillingness to tackle issues head on – people do not want to have difficult conversations.**

3. **People are unaware of how they come across and the impact it has on the conflict.**

4. **A general feeling of it will all just go away if left alone.**

Here is a useful exercise that helps get to the real cause of the issue(s)

On a flip chart write down the following in a table format:

Source of conflict	When does it happen	The response	'So What?'

The key is to look at the real source of the conflict(s) in your team and not just the things that manifest themselves on the surface. You could use a tool such as the 5 Whys to help get to the root cause.

The Five Whys

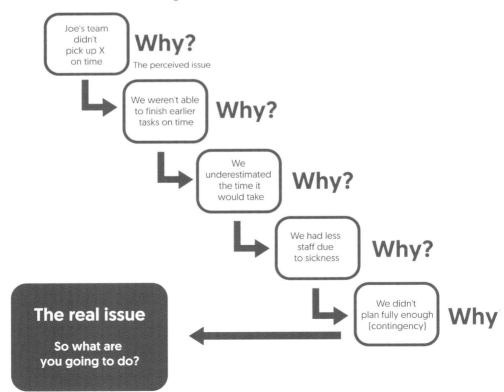

When does conflict tend to occur? Is it always on a Monday, at month end etc...? How do the team respond to these conflicts/issues as they arise and what wider impact does this have?

When you solve issues/conflicts, do you do so for the moment, or do you put in place systems for addressing these types of concerns in the future?

The 'So What' column is for you to capture what you are going to change from now on? Ask, 'So what can we do differently?'

This is a simple framework and in addition to this have a discussion as a team to understand what the individual and team triggers are that can lead to conflict and proactively look for ways that you can stop these triggers before they occur.

If conflict is present, do not fear tackling it head on. Creating this environment and way of being in a team can help with longer-term resiliency when the team is under pressure. This is another area I get asked about a lot, so let us take a look at resiliency.

Resiliency

We maintain our self-image and self-esteem relative to the positive or negative values associated with group/team membership and by comparing with other groups. Positive identity [feeling good] is largely based on comparisons, this idea is supported by Magda Arnold's appraisal theory [1960]. What this means is that the power of the collective team leads to higher levels of self-esteem and resiliency with its individual members. If you feel good/positive, then you are much more likely to remain more resilient. The culture of the team [chapter 1] effects how you feel, and your feelings effect the culture. Get the culture right to create stronger resiliency, both in individuals and as a collective. Strength in numbers but only if those numbers are made up of the right people with the right mind-set. If you set your team up for perennial success rather than quick fixes or easy wins then you will be more resilient as a team.

On a more personal note, stepping away slightly from the team context, I was asked recently what strategies I use to stay resilient in challenging times. I do not think I necessarily have strategies per se, I have a way of being and a way of thinking that helps me to stay grounded. There is no right or wrong and everyone is different.

Here are 5 things that help me:

 I was taught many years ago a resistance to interrogation technique that takes your mind to a different place, a good place, your own space. Sometimes I delve into that place as it really helps if things are starting to pile up a bit in my mind. To do this you simply need to find your own 'special place' - this can be something that you really enjoy doing or somewhere from your childhood that holds immensely happy memories for you.

There is an extreme example of this with the story of Major James Nesmeth who spent 7 years as a prisoner of war in Vietnam. His special place was the golf course and he visualised playing every day whilst held in captivity. When he set foot on a golf course again after not playing for over 7 years his game had massively improved. The golf (special place) is what kept him going through the dark times.

No one can tell you what your special place, or thing is but make it real and something that calms you. When things get bad and it is safe to do so, take yourself there – steady your breathing and let your mind only be in that place. Nothing else matters. At that point, you see, hear and feel nothing around you – you are completely immersed in your place. When I return from my place, I am much calmer and able to concentrate and move forward.

N**O**

Another great technique I use that is similar to some NLP tools is to imagine a time in your life when you were confident, assertive and resilient. Visualise this situation as if you were watching a film of it. Play the film to yourself and see your behaviour and imagine your thoughts at the time. If you cannot think of a situation that involves yourself, think of a person you believe is confident, assertive and resilient and picture their situation and behaviour. Play the film (visualisation) repeatedly and use a trigger word to remind you of the feeling and the situation. Your trigger word could be any word – but let us say it is the word 'resilient'. This is a great way to help reframe your thinking and see things in a different way.

N**O**

I also really enjoy gardening; it is a real passion of mine. Being in the garden and with nature is just so cathartic. There is something about it that has a huge calming effect on me and helps me to stay grounded. The fresh air, vitamin D, touch of earth running through your fingers and the look and feel of a garden as it flourishes is an immensely powerful natural medicine. If you do not like the idea of gardening maybe just try growing one thing in a pot - see how you get on. Gardening aside my biggest advice would always be to get outside - be at one with nature (it is up to you if you want to hug trees).

N<u>o</u>

I use the support I have around me – the ones I love and who love me. The importance of friends and family can never be underestimated.

Be open with your family and friends about how you are feeling and talk about it. Joke, sing, dance or just be in each other's virtual company. In times when I may be feeling a little low the sight of my daughter's or my son's smile on a video call always raises me back up. The same goes for your team if you have one. Use the strength of each other, lean on one another and truly support each other. Speak as regularly as you can and speak openly and honestly.

N<u>o</u>

Finally, I put things in perspective by thinking about times that I have been in worse situations before and more importantly, that there are many, many people a lot worse off than I am. I am incredibly lucky!

For example, I remember feeling particularly tired and homesick when I was on a training exercise in Kenya several years ago. I was driving with a couple of colleagues when we were flagged down by a local who pleaded with us to take their son to the local hospital to be treated for a snake bite.

The local hospital was 8km away – quite a distance for an injured young boy to walk or be carried by someone but in our Land Rover it would take little time.

We rushed this young boy to the local convent, which was also the hospital, his breathing had worsened, and my limited team medic training told me that it was not looking good. I had him in my arms and literally kicked the doors open and rushed in. Looking back, it was like a scene from a film – there should have been a large cinematic sound score playing as I entered. I handed the boy to the stunned nuns/nurses and went to comfort the father as best as I could.

Using our interpreter, I learned that the boy had been bitten by a snake not too far from his home while he was on his daily 5km walk to school. The family had no mode of transport and the 10km round trip walk to and from school took place every day.

An hour or so later one of the nurses came out to inform the father that the boy had died. That episode in my life taught me to never, ever take for granted what I have – things can always be worse. Ground yourself to find more resilience.

One last point that is relevant to resiliency is a reminder that you should always search for purpose over happiness. If you have a purpose you generally feel happier and as a result you are in a better position to tackle life's challenges. Imagine now the power of a collective team purpose!

Summary – Challenge

Every high performing team that I have built, operated in, or helped over the years has created a culture of challenge that helps to motivate the team members and to continue to move the team forwards.

Pushing people out of their comfort zone for short periods of time has been proven to help build confidence in individual ability and to strengthen a team as a result.

Everyone in a team should feel comfortable enough to challenge others but to also be challenged back. This is particularly important if you are a leader. Let your team challenge you. Doing this allows the team to build up a level of resiliency and trust that will help you resolve any conflict that arises in the team.

When a team is challenged and they work together towards success this creates pride, which in turn serves to drive the team onwards. The additional element that really creates sustained success is how the team supports each other when driving forward.

"Encourage, lift and strengthen one another. For the positive energy spread to one will be felt by us all. For we are connected, one and all."

Deborah Day

It is no good simply building a team and then letting them get on with it with no process in place to review and adapt accordingly. The team, including you, will need to be continually challenged and supported to maintain success and continue to improve. You must all ensure that you have each other's backs. It is important to review regularly to continually develop you and your team.

It is not just the large-scale big stuff that make a difference. Small wins build up and help to create a positive mind-set and a culture of success.

"One pen, one notebook and one teacher can change the world."

Malala Yousafzai

I love this quote from Malala who is such an inspirational lady!

This links to creating smaller strategies – little wins that lead to success. Think big but plan in smaller detail.

The ideal of course is to create an environment of high support and high challenge. I previously used the analogy of a building, let us revisit this idea. When a building is being constructed, the foundations are in place and then as each brick is bound to the next support is given so that it can sit properly and then settle. Sometimes the structure may need some scaffolding.

That building may then operate extremely successfully for a time but what happens when you build an extension to it? The scaffolding is re-introduced to add that support element as the change happens. People and teams are no different. If you are building your team you need the foundations in place and then ongoing support. If you have an established team but are introducing change – put in place the additional support needed.

A saying that we use at Successfactory™ is **speed up by slowing down**.

It is fine to step off the hamster wheel on occasion and step into the comfort zone – this helps to relieve stress (if we are pushed outside of our comfort zone into stress constantly it will lead to anxiety, fatigue and worse). Sometimes using a coaching approach helps move between comfort and performance. There is a plethora of information out there regarding coaching. Some of it good and some of it awful (in my opinion). In its basic form coaching is about using questions to solve problems/challenges. It uses a pull approach rather than a push (questions to pull answers from someone rather than simply giving them the answer that is in your own head and not necessarily the best answer).

Say THANK YOU to help build and support a high performing team

Why should you give thanks to others in the team? Have you ever stopped to give way to someone in another vehicle and as they pass there is not even an acknowledgement let alone a thank you from them? How did it make you feel?

Saying thank you, even for 'trivial' things can make a big difference to how people feel and behave. People who feel appreciated and respected are more motivated than those whose efforts go unrecognised. They tend to be much more engaged and committed to their teams because they know that they are making a difference (making a difference always scores highly on engagement surveys and questionnaires into what drives people to do the work that they do).

Thanking people can be more powerful than rewarding with monetary or material bonuses. Giving sincere praise helps to build good work relationships within a high performing team and cements the feeling of trust. It becomes a reciprocal thing where others are very willing to return the positivity – this creates a much better team dynamic and culture.

Praise has another amazing effect on human beings – it releases chemicals that make us feel good. When we receive genuine and sincere praise, our bodies release Dopamine. This is a neurotransmitter, and it is associated with feelings of happiness, pride, and fulfilment (all the things that we want and need in a high performing team). When you praise someone, you are assisting them to want to replicate that feeling again and again by carrying out the action that led to the praise (it feels good after all). Therefore, you are helping to create a sustained positive team culture.

Things that get in the way of praise

Some people find it exceedingly difficult to give praise. If they were brought up in an environment where this did not happen, it probably will not be their default to give praise to other people. Others can feel uncomfortable because for various reasons they feel embarrassed dishing out praise to others, especially in public.

If you struggle to give praise, try and discover why and take action to change this about yourself. Try and make it a conscious thing every day to recognise other people's good work and as uncomfortable as it may be for you – praise them. The more you do it, the easier it gets.

How to make praise more powerful

Try these ideas:

Do not go over the top

It is important to give praise but do not go over the top. If you praise all the time for every single little thing, it will lessen the impact of your praise and potentially you will come across as shallow or false to others.

Do not be vague

Have you ever heard praise such as "good job!" or "Well done, you are doing great!" While this is better than nothing, you will make more of an impact if you are more specific. Being specific cuts out any confusion.

Every time you praise people in your team, be specific about what they did and what impact their actions had. If you say, "Dave did a great job yesterday!" it is too vague.

For instance, you could say, "The way you laid out the graphs in that project report really helped me to deliver the update to the senior leadership team in a clear and concise way; thank you."

Involve in action

There are many ways that you can complement and praise others. Think back to the story of Fred in chapter 1. Involving people in your own challenges and coming up with actions together is a brilliantly subtle way of praising others as it says a lot about how much you trust and respect their experience, skills, and character. This is one of the reasons that having an inclusive decision-making process is so important to a high performing team.

Praise sincerely

When you praise others with sincerity, the rest of the team will very quickly learn what is important to you as a team member – it shows what your values are. Thinking back to the stages of team creation in chapter 1 the concept of sincere praise is especially relevant if you are trying to create a culture in a new team. This builds strong bonds and helps to create a level of trust.

Balance your praise with other feedback. The optimum ratio for performance is a 3:1 of positive to negative feedback. But do not get bogged down in numbers, the important thing is to always aim to give more positivity without losing sight of what needs to be improved – I am not saying gloss over the bad with all positive good stuff.

Praise everyone accordingly - Know the people in your team

Everyone in your team is different and their default setting for how they like to be praised will change according to different circumstances. Each team member will have different motivations (although many will be similar). You must know members of the team below just surface level. Getting to know your team's interests is so important if you are going to praise people accordingly (think back to intrinsic motivation and the story of Fred in chapter 1).

Some people love being the centre of attention and it motivates them more if they are praised publicly. Other team members may prefer a quiet "thank you" away from the crowd. It is important to analyse the best type of praise for each person.

Do not just praise the 'big stuff'

Do not think that only the major projects/tasks or your 'preferred' team members should receive your praise. This can lead to some people getting praised all the time – this may continue to drive them to perform well, but what about the rest of the team, you should try to include the quieter team members who get less recognition – this might be the thing that brings them out of their shell and motivated to do more. Remember the garden analogy in chapter 1? How even is your flower bed?

Praise the small things (without going overboard). Not everything has to be a big life changing event – I have always loved the quote from Anita Roddick:

"If you think you are too small to make a difference, sleep in a room with a mosquito."

Be consistent

Like parenting or training a dog, praise needs consistency. If you praise often for one week, and then do not praise at all for the next three weeks, you will create confusion in the team. Instead, create a consistent praise team culture.

Remember that it is NOT only a leader's job to dish praise out.

If you wait until your people are leaving the team or organisation to start praising them then it is too late. Make it a habit and a team 'cultural norm' to give genuine, and appropriate praise. It is common sense that people who feel recognised and appreciated are more likely to stay in a team than those who are not.

Keep a sense of humour to support and lift each other up

The military tend to be particularly good at this. I remember the dark humour present on operations that kept me, and the team going and really picked us up when we were at our lowest ebb. We used to make fun of each other regularly (usually about cleanliness or bodily functions) – for example, I was away from a Forward Operating Base (F.O.B) for a period of time and on my return my small sleeping area had been filled up with as much toothpaste, chewing gum and mouthwash as the lads could get hold of with a hand-written note saying "oi boss – sort your breath out, it's hacking!" (My team knew that I was obsessed with brushing my teeth no matter where I was in the world and I still am to this day).

The humour should be appropriate to the team and the situation and should never be offensive (pay attention to the protected 9 characteristics or you will have HR and the law breathing down your necks). Do not forget that everyone is different. What one person finds funny another will take offence at. We have all no doubt said something that has caused offence to somebody at some point. I know that I have. Try not to beat yourself up about it and make the effort to know everyone in your team well enough so that this does not happen.

One final thing I would like to share with you which is a brilliant tool to help support people and to problem solve at the same time. It is from the world of coaching and is called Masterminding. This is a great tool to use in team meetings or as and when issues arise.

Masterminding

1. Sit together as a team in a comfortable environment away from any distractions.

2. A member of the team will volunteer a challenge/issue/question to start the discussion. Something (anything) that they need support with.

3. The team will have 3 minutes to ask context building questions to help understand the owner's challenge.

4. At the end of the 3 minutes the owner of the question must move out of the group and sit in a chair with his/her back to the group. A notepad and pen will be useful at this point.

5. The remainder of the team have 10 minutes now to discuss out loud and openly how they would tackle the challenge or answer the question.

6. During the 10 minutes the owner of the question cannot contribute to the discussion.

7. At the end of the 10 minutes the owner will turn around and re-join the discussion. Using the notes that they made whilst listening they can then seek clarity of things that were said and then share either two things they are going to do as a result of the discussion or the two things that resonate with them the most.

This is an inclusive and powerful tool that helps to support individuals in a team and offer potential solution ideas to problems. Try it – see how you get on. Stick to the timings though – if you do not it has a habit of descending into a long and off the track conversation, which you can save for another occasion unless it is highly relevant and useful right now.

Some questions you can ask about support:

1. **How will you support each other and continue to use the most beneficial behaviours to ensure the team stays cohesive during any period of uncertainty?**

2. **How will you create the culture of 'I've got your back'?**

3. **What support processes and frameworks (scaffolding) do you have in place?**

4. **Does the team use praise effectively as a support and motivational tool?**

5. **Do you share a similar sense of humour in the team?**

Summary – Support

If you have spent a lot of energy, time, and money on building a team this will all go to waste if you forget the ongoing support that it will need to remain high performing.

It is not just about support during comfortable times – one could argue that this is relatively simple. The harder part is supporting each other when times are tough. Having the 'right people' with the 'right fit' to the culture of the team is imperative for this to be a core fundamental of the team.

Create the right culture for the team, recruit well, know each other, have processes in place, trust each other and tolerate mistakes that are made, and appreciate that everyone is different and understand what support every individual needs.

Continually check in with each other. Being in a high performing team is not about individuals working on their own, it is about the individuals banding together to achieve sustained collective success. This means parking any hindering egos.

Individual egos with their own agendas do not equal a high performing team.

THE IMPACT OF EGO ON A TEAM

"The personal ego already has a strong element of dysfunction, but the collective ego is, frequently, even more dysfunctional, to the point of absolute insanity."

Eckhart Tolle

In addition to the main chapters of this book I would like to add some ideas about ego and the impact it can have on a team.

If you are a leader then TRUST YOUR TEAM! Have I mentioned this before? That is because it is so, so important. Park your ego – it is not about how well you can 'manage' people. If you recruited intelligently and trained your team well and on top of that, you created the right environment/culture for success then let them get on with what they are good at. You cannot control everything. As a leader you keep your eye on the bigger picture, you strategise, plan and let your team deliver on the tasks that align to the overarching goal(s).

What is ego?

*   A person's sense of self-esteem or self-importance.

*   The "I" or self of a person that distinguishes itself from the selves of others.

*   The part of human psychology that experiences and reacts to the outside world and mediates between the primitive drives of the id (the part of the mind in which innate and instinctive impulses are processed) and the demands of the social and physical environment. According to Sigmund Freud's psychoanalytic theory of personality, the id is the personality component made up of unconscious psychic energy that works to satisfy basic urges, needs, and desires

*   A person's level of self-importance, self-esteem, or self-image.

We all have an ego and understanding it and knowing how to use everyone's ego effectively is key in a high performing team. If you do not then team cohesion will fall apart quickly, and long-term success will not be found. I have witnessed this on several occasions, for example, I was asked to work with a senior leadership team a few years ago who had some challenges, to put it politely. Most of their challenges could be dealt with and resolved effectively so that they could operate much more efficiently as an SLT, but there was one area that proved to be their biggest challenge and that was their MD (the 'boss'). The guy was simply not in the right role and had a negative ego the size of a planet.

To give you an example of what I mean, we would run facilitated discussions involving everyone in the room allowing input from each person and this guy would simply get up and wander around not paying attention. When it came to me facilitating (leading) a discussion because I wanted to introduce a tool that could help the team he simply stood up, walked behind where I was sat and then just stood there. Strange and disruptive behaviour, which given that they (he) was paying me for my services made it even more weird. He kept interrupting so I decided to take a break and took him to one side to have a chat.

This was all about ego – the guy simply could not let his go for the sake of the team. He was the 'boss' and boy did he let everyone know it. Many of the team came up to me separately and apologised for him and said, "that's just the way he is". **This is not an excuse at all.** Think back to chapter 1 about culture. Every team member either changes or perpetuates a culture.

A culture of enlarged egos and 'I am the top dog' mentality will NEVER succeed in the long run. It will cause resentment, unhealthy rivalry, and competition within a team. And as mentioned previously, some of the inability to truly use innovative ideas from new blood in a business is down to fear and ego.

An area that gets talked about a lot in more recent times is emotional intelligence. This is key to understanding your ego and how it affects others. Remember that it is the ripple effect that is most important.

So, what is emotional intelligence?

"The ability to understand the way people feel and react and to use this skill to make good judgements and to avoid or solve problems".
And...
*"The ability to understand and control your own feelings, and to understand the feelings of others and react to them in a suitable way".**

* The Cambridge Dictionary - https://dictionary.cambridge.org

At Successfactory™ we explain emotional intelligence by using the 5 Ss:

Self-Awareness: the ability to know one's emotions, strengths, weaknesses, drivers, values and goals and recognise how they impact on others while using gut feelings to guide decisions.

Questions for self-awareness:

1. **Do you know your emotional triggers?**

2. **Do you know your strengths? These are your natural strengths and not what you force yourself to do because it says so on your job specification.**

3. **Are you open and honest about your weaknesses? Your ego may be pushing them under the carpet as it does not want to admit them to anyone else.**

4. **What values do you live by?**

5. **How much do you consider other people when setting your own goals?**

Self-management: involves controlling or redirecting one's hindering or unhelpful emotions and impulses.

Questions for self-management:

1. **What tools and techniques do you employ to control your emotions and behaviours?**

2. **Do you find that you react differently to different people? If so, why, and what impact does this have?**

3. **Do you operate on impulse or are you more self-controlled and give thought to everything you do? What is the advantage and disadvantage of both?**

Social Skills: the multi-faceted skill of interacting with different people and managing relationships to move people in the desired direction.

Questions to ask about social skills:

1. Do you ever stop and analyse how you interact with others?

2. Does the way you use your social skills have a helpful or hindering effect on the team?

3. How could you possibly improve your relationships?

Here are some useful visual tools to start the ball rolling. Jot some ideas down.

Who are Your Key Relationships; Both Internally and Externally?

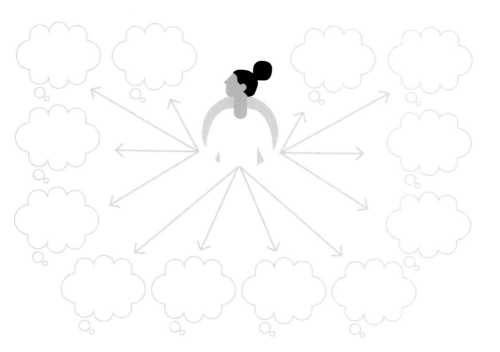

Key Relationships to Build...

Name/Position/Area	Improvement Needed	Actions I Need to Take to Improve

Social Awareness: empathy, considering other people's feelings especially when making decisions.

Questions to ask about social awareness:

1. Do you stop and really make a point of understanding what is going on around you?

2. Do you listen to words only or do you try and read between the lines?

3. Do you care about people's feelings or is it all about the task?

Social Adaptability: Willingness to change your approach to drive desired outcomes, to re-prioritise when business needs override your own.

Some questions to ask about social adaptability:

1. **Do you tend to use a one-stop-shop approach?**

2. **Do you always understand the business needs?**

3. **How could you be more adaptable with your approach?**

Some final questions about ego for you to consider:

1 . **Do you understand how your own ego drives how you operate and interact with people?**

2. **How do the different egos in the team work together?**

3. **How can you use the egos in your team to shape a helpful culture?**

Summary – Ego

Whether you are a leader or a team member you MUST park your ego for the sake of the team and the shared goals. If you cannot do this, then get out of the team and be a lone wolf. This way, you and your ego will get on just fine.

Egos that are hindering a team's success need to be challenged. Using an exercise like the one outlined in chapter 1 can help with this. It is no excuse for a team to moan about people's egos and not challenge them. Egos feed into and influence a culture; if your cultural foundation is not how you need it to be then you will not sustain high performance, you will become frustrated and inevitably fail.

We all have an ego. Just do not let them derail a team's success. A high performing team is not about the individual.

Final Thoughts
So, there it is.

1. Culture & People

Create the right culture for your team and commit to a compelling Vision

Understand that people are different and use this to the team's advantage

2. Strategy & Process

Do not rely on long-term strategy planning

Have clearly defined, simple processes and get them 100% right but adapt them when necessary

3. Truth & Trust

Truth ALWAYS

Have trust in each other and in what happens when things don't go to plan

4. Knowledge & Decisions

Do not pretend to know everything

Use inclusive and flexible decision-making processes

5. Actions & Mistakes

Actions not just words

Have tolerance of mistakes

Do-Review-Understand

Strive to learn and keep moving forward

6. Challenge & Support

Challenge people but also give them permission to challenge back

Create an environment of mutual support

Now it is time to go and put it all into practice in your own worlds. Add to it, adapt it and make it real to you but...do something!

Here are a few concluding thoughts from me to see you on your way to success:

1. **Be focused – develop a sense of purpose that everyone is passionate about and be true to it. Constantly evaluate it and adapt, as necessary.**

2. **Be confident in the skills, experience, and expertise within the team (if you need more – get more).**

3. **Understand self-limiting beliefs and comfort zones – challenge them and push each other outside of them regularly. Be honest with each other about who you really are and do not expend energy trying to be something you are not.**

4. **Work to a plan. Be committed to each element of the plan including the self-discipline about identifying and delivering the detail (even the bits you do not like) – daily, weekly and monthly, but always keep in the back of your mind that no plan survives contact with the enemy (things happen – roll with it).**

5. **Build on strengths and follow a team action plan that capitalises on them.**

6. **Work hard but do not forget to play – increase your knowledge, be willing to learn from others and from mistakes. Be creative and innovative – if things are not working try another way.**

7. **As a collective take ownership for achieving the outcomes you want. Do not expect things to simply happen – create belonging.**

8. **Be resilient, be persistent and act.**

5 Top Tips on Team Dynamics that I learnt from the military that cross over to all teams

1. Make the team structure and hierarchy as flat as possible – not only are things more transparent but it is quicker to communicate.

2. Where possible cross train everyone to be capable of doing each job within the team. If this is not possible then at least make sure that everyone has an idea of what each other/other departments do. What is vital is that you decentralise decision-making to the lowest capable level.

3. Know every member of the team on a human level. Remember that teams are about people and not just processes. It is also worth remembering that if you mix good people with bad processes, the processes will usually win.

4. Recruit intelligently and then trust people to do the job (even without a leader present). If you cannot build trust, your leadership is obsolete, and you need to have the courage to realise this and move out of the way.

5. Finally – and most importantly, leave your ego at the door.

A high performing team excites, challenges, supports, motivates, and empowers every member.

It is challenging work to get a team to a high performing level and then sustain that excellence. There may be tough times, but they will not last forever. Persevere – it is worth it.

"Figure out what you're passionate about and work hard. There is no substitution for dedication."

Mary Barra, CEO of General Motors

I hope that this book has made you think and has opened up some interesting conversations for your team.

Now it is over to you.

I wish you every success in the future.

Cheers!

Dave

Recommended Reading

Leadership Laid Bare
Graham Wilson. [Success Online Publishing]

Strategies of the Serengeti
Stephen Berry. [Neo Publishing]

Go MAD – The Art of Making A Difference
 Andy Gilbert. [Go MAD Books]

Black Box Thinking
Matthew Syed. [John Murray Publishers]

The Culture Code
Daniel Coyle. [Random House Business Books]

Our Iceberg is Melting
John Kotter. [Macmillan]

The Naked Leader
David Taylor. [Bantam Books]

The Social Animal
David Brooks. [Random House Publishing]

The Pressure Principle
Dr Dave Alred MB. [Penguin]

Shackleton's Way
Margot Morrell and Stephanie Capparell. [Nicholas Brealey Publishing]

All pictures and quotes in this book are the author's own unless otherwise stated.